City of beauty, reformation and pioneering research

David Berkley

Day One

Series Editor: Brian H Edwards

Cambridge
City of beauty, reformation and pioneering research

CONTENTS

© Day One Publications 2008   First printed 2008   Reprinted 2015

A CIP record is held at The British Library   ISBN 978-1-84625-119-1

Published by Day One Publications Ryelands Road, Leominster, HR6 8NZ

℗ 01568 613 740 FAX 01568 611 473 email: sales@dayone.co.uk www.dayone.co.uk   All rights reserved

Design: Kathryn Chedgzoy   Produced by Polskabook, Poland

Welcome to Cambridge

For centuries Cambridge had been an avenue for radical ideas arriving from the continent, with the Benedictines and the friar orders playing a role in the university's early life. Although today Cambridge is world-famous for its pioneering science, it was the Reformation which put the city firmly on the map. The ideas of Erasmus and Luther shaped the thinking of so many Cambridge men who later died for their faith. Cambridge, the cradle of the English Reformation, also produced a host of Puritans including John Harvard who established the now famous university in America. Later Oliver Cromwell became MP for Cambridge which lay in the Parliamentarian heartland, and soon afterwards Isaac Newton started a scientific revolution, transforming the way the universe was understood.

Although the Wesleyan Evangelical Revival hardly touched Cambridge, Charles Simeon, a later evangelical, revived the ministry in England and launched young men as missionaries overseas. Wilberforce, another Cambridge man, led the fight against slavery, and Romantic poets like Wordsworth reacted to the Age of Reason and looked to nature for hope, whereas Darwin, hunting bugs round Cambridge, thought of nature as self-sufficient. However, at the Cavendish Laboratory, Clerk Maxwell saw no conflict between faith and scientific research.

Cambridge and its surrounding area now boasts Europe's fastest growing region of hi-tech; yet the weekly church attendance is significantly above the national average. Certainly religion and science are the heart of the Cambridge story.

Given the city's history of international importance and its sumptuous architecture it is small wonder that millions of tourists visit each year.

Facing page: *King's College Chapel; its verticality and enlarged windows are a hallmark of the Perpendicular style*

❶ Marshes, monasteries and medieval beliefs

Before the foundation of Cambridge University, foreign invasions each left their mark on the town which became strategically important on the edge of the Fens—a watery wilderness. Later, the local monks and friars all contributed to the teaching of the earliest students

The melting of the last ice age caused sea levels to rise dramatically so that the sea known today as the North Sea became far larger. Over what is now the Fens there stretched a huge expanse of water punctuated by many islands; the marshes surrounding them scarcely ever dried out except in drought conditions. Eventually the local economy of those who inhabited the islands of this region revolved around fishing, fowling and reed cutting. However, long before that, the invasion of England by various people had left its mark on the Fens and its inhabitants. First came the Romans, who started to drain a limited area of the wetlands to the north-east of Cambridge, digging canals called 'lodes' to help the drainage. The village of Lode still exists near Burwell. In Cambridge the old Roman road, the Via Devana, linking Colchester with Lincoln and Chester (known by the Romans as Castra Deva) and, lying beneath the modern Hills Road which approaches from the south-east, crossed the river Cam by a ford at the site now occupied by Magdalene Bridge; it then continued up Castle Hill before heading further north-west to Godmanchester and Huntingdon. Another Roman road, Akeman Street, linked the region north of Salisbury Plain with Brancaster, a harbour on the Norfolk coast through which the Romans brought in supplies from the continent. This road crossed Via Devana outside the Roman camp and close to the modern Shire Hall on Castle Hill. Successive waves of Anglo-Saxons filled the void left by the departing Romans. It was the Anglo-Saxons around AD 500 who established the town market which we see today. Three hundred years later, they also built the first Cambridge bridge—the Great Bridge— spanning the river where the Roman ford had been.

In AD 875 the Vikings arrived on the tide by long-ship. Not until the 17th century when the Fens were drained and a huge sluice

Facing page: The huge screen in King's Chapel with its organ loft and the world's largest fan vault overhead

Above: Ely Cathedral from the south

Left: Ely Cathedral—the 'Ship of the Fens'—seen across flood-waters where once the ancient abbey stood

Island tranquillity and a diet of eels

The first Benedictine monks appeared in the region in the seventh century. Just as St Anthony and the Desert Fathers had appreciated the solitude of the Egyptian desert for a life of prayer and contemplation, so the Benedictines viewed the Fenland islands as havens offering the tranquillity they sought. Soon they started to build their monasteries on several of these islands. However, they were not totally isolated since the islands lay at a relatively short distance from each other, and Cambridge represented a central point for them and 'terra firma'—although Cambridge itself was marshy in many places. It was Etheldreda, Queen of the East Angles, who founded Ely monastery in AD 673, but numerous others were built, for example at Thorney, Croyland, Ramsey and Walden. The 'Isle of Ely' by which Ely used to be known, reminds us of its watery origins, the name 'Ely' deriving from an old Saxon word for the natural breeding grounds of eels; these formed a substantial part of the local diet. According to the medieval 'Croyland Chronicle' the inhabitants of the small hamlet of Stuntney caught some 26,000 eels in one year alone.

built at Denver, north of Ely, did the river cease to be tidal as far as Cambridge. For centuries a boat could arrive close to the town from the north over a wide arc and only enter the actual river Cam at Waterbeach, some eight miles downstream from Cambridge. Once at Cambridge, the Vikings settled on the town's south bank, eventually building a river harbour just downstream from the Great Bridge. In Bridge Street, St Clement's Church still stands as a reminder of the Viking presence—though later rebuilt in stone—St Clement being the patron saint of Danish seafarers. In the Middle Ages considerable quantities of exports, especially of wool, passed through the Viking harbour bound for Europe's northern ports.

The Normans reached Cambridge the year after the Battle of Hastings. They built a motte and

Above: The Shire Hall now occupies part of the site of the Norman Castle and subsequent county gaol

bailey castle on the hill to the north of Great Bridge and close to the former site of the Roman camp, where it dominated both town and river. Two hundred years later the castle was reinforced in stone.

The river was the life-blood of Cambridge until recent times. Most supplies, including the lime-stone rocks destined for King's College Chapel, whose walls and vault were built between 1448 and 1515, arrived by barge. In AD 1211 King John gave a charter for a fair to be held annually on Stourbridge Common, the proceeds going to support the leper hospital run by Austin Canons at Barnwell, now an eastern suburb of the city. This common lies alongside the south bank of the Cam; ships could therefore discharge their merchandise direct onto the

Above: St Clement's Church with its 19th century tower; it is now used by the Greek Orthodox Church

Fair ground itself. For centuries Stourbridge Fair was the biggest in Europe—finally closing as recently as 1934—and merchants throughout Europe came to buy and sell there. It was here too that Isaac Newton bought a prism which he later used to refract light; it is suggested that the fair may have inspired the episode of 'Vanity Fair' which appears in John Bunyan's Pilgrim's Progress. Apart from the leper hospital

and the usual medieval hospices and hostels common to most medieval towns, there was also the 'Hospital of St John' run by Augustinians on the site now occupied by St John's College. Just outside the southern boundary of the medieval town stood the 'Hospital of St. Anthony and St. Eloi' for the mentally ill. The current St Eligius Street runs through the precincts of the former hospital, Eligius being a pseudonym for St. Eloi, patron

Top left: Stourbridge Common today; the streets to the immediate south bear the names of alleys on the old fair ground, e.g. Garlic Row and Oyster Row

Left: St Mary Magdalene's Church, the 'Leper Chapel', close to Stourbridge Common

Above: St John's College First Court showing the remains in the lawn of the chapel of the earlier Hospital of St John

saint of metal-workers (for 'Eloi' read 'alloy'). As for the many medieval churches, these too were major landmarks in the town, with the Church of St. Botolph, patron saint of travellers, tucked just inside Trumpington Gate at its southern end, whilst St Giles Church lay close to its northern perimeter just beyond Great Bridge, St. Giles being patron saint of the blind and of lepers. St Bene't's Church, commemorating St Benedict and built by Saxons in AD 1030, has a tower from which the Saxon rebel Hereward the Wake kept watch on the advancing Normans. Inside the church a plaque commemorates Fabian Stedman who instituted campanology in the 17th century, whilst Thomas Hobson of 'Hobson's Choice' is buried in the chancel. Hobson, the proprietor of nearby stables, chose the horse irrespective of a rider's experience or size; invariably he chose the freshest horse and tethered it at the stable entrance and these 'misfits' became the source of mirth all round. (see also page 71 for his more positive contribution to Cambridge).

'Christian Heritage'
Among the current displays on view within the Round Church, which is administered by Christian Heritage (see Travel Information), there is a copy of the *Canterbury Gospels*, the oldest illustrated Bible manuscript in the world. Written on vellum and in Latin, the original came to England in AD 601 with St Augustine of Rome. It was

Top: St Bene't's Church, built by the Saxons in 1030, is the oldest extant building in the county

Bottom: The Round Church standing beside the former Roman road, the Via Devana

The Church of the Holy Sepulchre—now the Round Church

At the apex formed between the top of the former High Street, now the northern extension of King's Parade, and the Via Devana, now Bridge Street, stood the Church of the Holy Sepulchre; it was built in AD 1130 by members of the 'Fraternity of the Holy Sepulchre' not, as is sometimes supposed, the Knights Templar who only arrived from the continent as the building neared completion. The 'Fraternity' consisted of Austin Canons (similar to Augustinians) and crusaders returning from the first crusade to Jerusalem where they had seen The Church of the Holy Sepulchre built by the Roman Emperor Constantine and his mother Helena; it stands, supposedly, directly over the site of the Resurrection. The Cambridge building, now known locally as the Round Church, served initially as a wayfarers' chapel or oratory. Travellers wishing to pray for personal safety as they journeyed would enter such chapels, where priests or monks serving as intermediaries between God and man interceded on their behalf; it was believed that God accepted prayer through them alone. The chapel later became a parish church and was extended after the Black Death (1348) as were so many churches. In the 15th century stained glass was fitted; the windows previously were without glass and open to the sky. Bells too were installed in a redesigned roof. However, this proved too heavy and the entire roof collapsed in 1841.

saved at the Dissolution of the Monasteries by Matthew Parker who later became Archbishop of Canterbury. The original is kept in Corpus Christi College, never leaving except for an Archbishop's enthronement. Parker completed the Elizabethan Settlement (see chapter 4) on the authority of the church alone, but in 1572 the 'Admonition Controversy' began, marking a new phase in the struggle with the Puritans which required him to probe into what might be termed 'other people's business'—hence the saying 'Nosey Parker'.

The University and early friars

In AD 1209 riots between 'town and gown' at Oxford led to fatalities and to the temporary closure of that university (see in this series *Travel through Oxford—City of saints, scholars and dreaming spires* by Andrew Atherstone). Some of the students and their teachers came to Cambridge, drawn apparently by the teaching already provided

Above: *The nave of Cambridge's Round Church where travellers stood in prayer*

Left: *The Round Church's east window with Christ, fully alive (his eyes are wide open), crucified on the Tree of Life*

Above: *The Canterbury Gospels, the world's oldest illustrated Bible manuscript, open at Luke's Gospel*

at Cambridge by the abbots of the outlying monasteries. Older monks gave lectures to younger monks and novices in wooden barns on the outskirts of the town. The newcomers from Oxford took advantage of this it would seem, and once here they decided to stay. No university or college buildings had yet been built, but those arriving found accommodation where they could. Thus Cambridge University came into existence in 1209 and it was not long before the friar orders arrived in town as well. A religious house was founded

in 1226 by the Franciscans on the site now occupied by Sidney Sussex. Twelve years later the Dominicans followed on the site now used by Emmanuel College, and later that century the Carmelites settled where Queens' College now stands and the Austin Friars settled near the town centre. Whilst the University of Oxford marginally predates that of Cambridge in terms of its earliest buildings, it was Cambridge in 1318 which first received the all-important charter granting papal recognition. As for the construction of university and

Above: An 18th century view along
Trumpington Street, with (left)
Peterhouse, the first college to be
founded (1284)

college buildings, the first to
appear were certain colleges, the
university officers continuing
to administer university affairs
from the rooms they hired in
town. Eventually the building
which housed the university
headquarters, later known as
the Regent House, was built
in the second half of the 14th
century with the Divinity School
on the ground floor. These are

Above: The north transept of Jesus College chapel, earlier a Benedictine nunnery
church, with the blocked up doorway through which the nuns entered from their
dormitories at night to attend worship

still university buildings though their usage has changed. Fuller reference is made in chapter 5 to King's College Chapel, a building famed throughout the world for the sheer beauty of its architecture, its stained glass and its televised service of Christmas carols, but here it is appropriate to mention its screen. It was completed in 1536 and built of bog oak—oak that has lain for long in water, the resultant effect being both to harden and to darken it. The screen was Henry VIII's inspiration, built in imitation of the stone-built triumphal arches of Roman Emperors, particularly that of Constantine in Rome. The purpose of church screens (the rood screen)—and before the Reformation all churches had them—was to partition off the chancel, the priest and his acolytes (assistants to the priest, often in training), from the congregation in the nave, thereby screening the most sacred part of the church from the sins of those who entered the west end. This was another example of medieval beliefs which were abandoned by the Protestant Reformers in the 16th and 17th centuries. The German reformer, Martin Luther maintained that a priest's function was to expound the Scriptures and perform the sacraments and that in themselves priests were neither better nor worse than others, and that anyone could worship and pray to God directly, providing they had true faith and lived in a right relationship with God.

Above: *Jesus College: the entrance to the chapter house of the former Benedictine nunnery*

The Medieval outlook and 'superstition'

Life expectancy in the Middle Ages was short because of war, famine and plague, and people had no real belief in their capacity to improve the human condition. They looked to a better life in the hereafter, focusing on God and the church and hoping the latter would help them reach the former. The church increased its wealth at the expense of the poor. It also built its image round the medieval beliefs that became part of everyday life, such as the need for intermediaries in prayer and the regular partitioning of church buildings through the use of rood screens. Over the centuries these and other medieval superstitions proliferated, including the installation of saints' relics deemed to make a holy place even holier, and priestly auricular (oral) confession, penance and absolution; chantry chapels were built by the wealthier members of society in which priests and monks sang (chanted) Requiem Masses and prayers for the souls of the departed to expedite their progress through purgatory. From the sale of indulgences (a certificate of pardon for a price) the money paid by the purchaser went ostensibly, but often not at all, to help finance some enterprise such as the building of a cathedral or the launch of a crusade; in return, the purchaser was guaranteed their soul's speedy transit through purgatory after death. Other beliefs included transubstantiation whereby the Eucharistic bread and wine translates in a mystical way into Christ's body and blood.

This led to the Reformation concept of the 'priesthood of all believers'. Starting from that premise people then argued that if priests were no more special than members of their congregations, were kings necessarily more worthy in God's eyes than their subjects? The roots of democracy are in fact grounded in the Reformation; one has only to compare the English constitutional monarchy with the French autocracy of the 18th century for this to be obvious.

There were undoubtedly aspects of the church in the middle ages which were greatly beneficial to society, including the appearance of the earliest secular universities which emerged from the monasteries but were still dominated by the church; hospitals, hospices and hostels were run by monks and friars to help the sick and elderly, as well as travellers seeking accommodation. Individual monasteries and religious establishments underpinned local economies, and the mighty Norman and Gothic cathedrals were an inspiration to every inhabitant in the land. Sadly, however, the church was at fault both morally and intellectually. The misguided actions of the crusaders, the iniquity of the Inquisition, and the cruelty of subsequent slavery were all wholly incompatible with the Christianity taught by Jesus Christ.

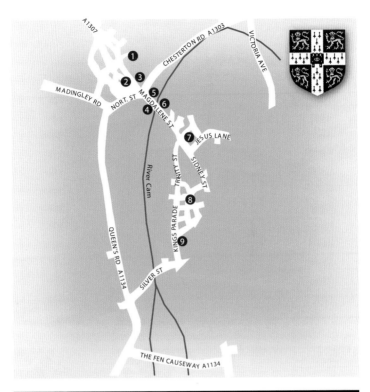

CAMBRIDGE: FROM CASTLE HILL AND QUAYSIDE TO ITS CENTRE

KEY

1 CASTLE MOUND &
   SHIRE HALL
2 ST. PETER'S CHURCH

3 ST. GILE'S CHURCH
4 THE PICKEREL INN
5 MAGDALENE COLLEGE
6 QUAYSIDE

7 THE ROUND CHURCH
8 MARKET SQUARE
   (MARKET HILL)
9 ST. BENET'S CHURCH

Above: *Magdalene College from Quayside*

TRAVEL INFORMATION

Castle Mound and St Peter's Church

Castle Mound, linked with the Norman Castle and the Roman Camp to the immediate west, makes a good starting point affording fine views over Cambridge. Descend towards the river, making a slight detour to the right to reach the tiny St Peter's Church. Its key is normally held at the nearby art museum, Kettles Yard. The exterior of the south wall was once repaired using Roman tiles found close by. A fine Norman font greets the eye inside.

Top: The punt station at Magdalene Bridge: the punts are the descendants of barges which brought merchandise to the town; water transport was the normal practice before road surfaces were improved

Above: The Norman St Peter's Church, rebuilt in part using Roman tiles found on the site

If time allows, and if it's open, take a quick look at the stained glass in St Giles Church on the other side of Castle Street.

Magdalene College

Magdalene Street, Cambridge, CB3 0AG
www.magd.cam.ac.uk
✆ 01223 332100

This site previously housed a Benedictine monks' hospice erected by the Abbot of Croyland in 1428, and attended by young monks from Croyland, Ely, Ramsey, Walden and other abbeys. In 1483 the hospice was transformed into Buckingham College involving both the 2nd and 3rd Dukes of Buckingham. It was refounded as Magdalene College in 1542 by Thomas Lord Audley of Walden who became Lord Chancellor of England in 1533 and who changed the pronunciation to 'Maudlin' to reflect his own name, often arrogantly spelling the college 'M-Audley-N'. The Magdalene College dining hall displays portraits and coats of arms in its stained glass recalling many famous alumni, whilst the chapel has its original roof. This was Samuel Pepys' college (chapter 5) and the library housing his collection, including his diary, is of great interest. Magdalene played a role second only to St John's in the story of the abolition of slavery, whilst many late 18th and early 19th century missionaries studied here, as did Charles Kingsley, the Christian Socialist (chapter 7). A.C. Benson, writer of 'Land of Hope and Glory', inspired a revival in college fortunes in the early 20th century whilst C.S. Lewis (chapter 8) was a Fellow of the College between 1954 and 1963.

Above: *The view along Magdalene Street with the 16th century Pickerel Inn on the right (blue facade)*

Pickerel Inn

30 Magdalene St,
Cambridge
www.cambridge-pubs.
co.uk
✆ 01223 355068

Situated in the old
'red light' district
of town, it is the oldest
pub in Cambridge. Other
possible lunch stops and
restaurants lie along
Magdalene Street and in
Bridge Street.

Quayside and Magdalene Bridge

The Cambridge story
began here. This is
where the Romans forded
the river and the Saxons
built the first bridge.
The Viking harbour lay
some 100–150 metres
downstream from this
point.

The Round Church

The Round Church Vestry,
Bridge Street, Cambridge,
CB2 1UB
www.christian
heritageuk.org.uk
✆ 01223 311602

For historical details
see page 12. The
history of Cambridge
video 'Saints & Scholars'
is played continuously
each day. Another
video commemorates
the bi-centenary of the

Above: *The corner of 'Market Hill' (the Market
Square) with Great St Mary's beyond, and 'Peas
Hill', the site of the original fish market, to the
immediate left ('Peas' deriving from the Latin
'pisca' = fish)*

official Abolition of the Slave Trade in 1807, very much a Cambridge story. Twelve display boards explain the chronological development of the western world with its Christian roots. Guided tours are available, lasting approximately 1¾ hours, and include entry to several of the following colleges: St John's, Trinity College, Trinity Hall, Sidney Sussex, Jesus and Magdalene. They focus on the Christian heritage of Cambridge, which itself is a window on the evolution of European and North American society; in explaining the huge impact of Christianity on the West, they highlight values which need to be reclaimed in an increasingly sterile and rudderless society. No pre-booking is needed for these tours, though pre-booking for private groups can be arranged.

Market Hill

At the town centre, this market square, first built by the Saxons around AD 500, is open every day of every week, with rare exceptions. Individual stalls determine their start and finishing hours. There is no 'hill' though the name suggests one; the Saxon word for 'hill' also meant firm ground, a reminder that parts of Cambridge itself were marshy. Numerous medieval fires which destroyed parts of the town, including the churches of Holy Trinity and St Edward's in 1174 and Great St Mary's in 1290, were caused when stall-holders' braziers were knocked over and sparks ignited neighbouring thatched roofs.

St Bene't's Church

See page 11 for historical details. The limestone blocks at the corners of its tower laid first vertically then horizontally—known technically as 'long and short' work—are a clear indication of the work of Saxon stonemasons.

Above: Magdalene College

DES ❖ ERASMUS

❷ 'Erasmus laid the egg that the Reformers hatched'

By the Middle Ages the Christian church was seen by many as morally corrupt, but it took the Dutch scholar Erasmus in Cambridge to highlight its intellectual corruption and to seek its renewal from within; Luther and many other Reformers did so from without

Historians agree that had the Renaissance never occurred a Reformation would still have taken place within the Christian Church, though not necessarily when it did nor following the form it took. That said, the Renaissance had an enormous impact on the Reformation.

The achievements of the ancient Greeks and Romans had largely been obscured in the Western world following the 5th century barbarian invasions and the Dark Ages which resulted. The Renaissance (meaning 'rebirth') was partially inspired by the recovery of ideas emanating from the Greeks and Romans through 14th century literary giants like Petrarch and Boccaccio as well as artists such as Giotto. The architectural achievements of Brunelleschi are further evidence of a change in outlook leading to a change in style and expression. However the Renaissance also drew significantly on the early scientific achievements of the Arab world. The Arabs were also the vehicle whereby knowledge of many Greco-Roman texts later reached Europe: after looting the great library of Alexandria and other book stores in their conquests, they brought many of these texts from North Africa into Spain in the early 8th century. There they forced the local Jews, the intelligentsia, to translate them into Arabic, enabling the Jews to convey copies of the original to the rest of Europe. Many of these texts came to light in the 11th century when the Moors were driven south and Toledo, the old Visigothic capital, fell into Christian hands again. Soon after, the earliest universities started to appear, offering a somewhat more secular education than their monastic counterpart, albeit still under the Church's domination.

Above: *The entrance to Trinity Hall*

Facing page: *Erasmus portrayed in the stained glass of the reformation window in Trinity College Chapel*

The High Renaissance

The High Renaissance was sparked in 1453 when Constantinople fell to the Ottoman Turks, an event which marked the end of the old Eastern Roman/Byzantine Empire. The scholars in Constantinople escaped westwards before the city fell, and settled for the most part in Venice, Florence and other cities in northern Italy, bringing with them knowledge gained from their scholarship and research into the writings and philosophies of both the ancient Greco-Roman secular writers, and the Scriptures and writings of the early Church Fathers. They also brought the texts they had worked on which had never been seen before in Western Europe. At that point the Western world woke up: if the ancients had achieved what they had, why should not 15th century man do so as well? Suddenly the medieval focus on God and Church altered to accommodate the human being. A human-centred perspective came about, and the term 'humanism' emerged to define an emphasis on the promotion of human endeavour in all fields on the back of human achievement in the past. Unlike the modern use of the word,

Above: The world (the shaded area only between black lines) as known to Europeans in 1450

the 16th century term was in no sense anti-God, nor did it deny religious beliefs and values. This study of the past and its practical projection onto the contemporary scene became known as the 'New Learning', a term that also indicated a new educational method contrasting with medieval 'scholasticism'.

The new perspective coincided with the births of Leonardo da Vinci and Michelangelo followed by the exploratory voyages of Columbus and Vasco da Gama. The world was opening up, and Man was making it happen. The 'New Learning' of the

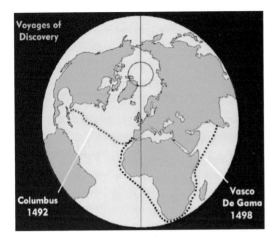

Renaissance would have achieved little, however, without the advent of printing in 1455 in Mainz, when Gutenberg printed the first book in Europe—the *Gutenberg Bible*. Caxton set up his printing press in London in 1476, but that twenty year gap meant that England was significantly behind the rest of Europe.

Bottom left: The exterior wall of the original court of Corpus Christi and its link to St Bene't's Church

Above: The world opens up: the voyages of Columbus and Vasco da Gama

Below: The 19th century main entrance and, beyond, the chapel of Corpus Christi designed by William Wilkins

The growth of the university

In Cambridge, the University was growing, if only slowly. The Black Death, which in 1348 had killed one third of the town's population, led to the founding

Above: Queens' College Cloister Court, seen through a cloister arch

of Trinity Hall in 1350 by Bishop Bateman of Norwich, and also to that of Corpus Christ College two years later by two of the town's

Above: The Old Dining Hall, Queens' College

guilds. The latter came about directly as a result of the plague, and the priority of the Master and its Fellows was to pray on behalf of the grieving townsfolk for the souls of those they had lost—it was believed that prayer offered for souls in purgatory by those alive would expedite the souls' progress to heaven. Only as a secondary consideration were the Master and Fellows of Corpus Christi to give instruction to the young pupils who came daily to the college gates.

In the earlier centuries students often arrived aged 12 to 14 and had to be educated to a minimum level before starting a degree course. They lived exclusively in the town where they were exposed to profiteering landlords and immoral influences. The total student numbers were only

Above: Jesus College 'chimney' (french 'chemin') and entrance

finally accommodated in colleges or their hostels in the 1540s, and by then other colleges such as King's, Queens', St Catherine's and Jesus, Christ's and St John's had been founded. Many of the earlier colleges resembled small monasteries with cloistered courts, and the life of Fellows and students followed very similar lines to those of a monastic order, though marginally more relaxed. Modern gowns derive from the clerical and monastic dress worn in those days; meals in college were often taken in silence unless Latin was permitted. Daily chapel attendance was obligatory though less frequent than in monasteries. The first thing studied was always the Bible

John Fisher

The University Chancellor in the early 1500s was John Fisher. He had been educated in the medieval scholastic tradition and though zealous to introduce the New Learning and its humanistic methodology onto the University curriculum, neither he nor any other lecturer in England was equipped to do so. Somebody therefore had to be imported, and in 1510 Fisher invited Desiderius Erasmus from Rotterdam to become Professor of Theology. For clarification of the term 'scholasticism', see in this series *Travel through Oxford* by Andrew Atherstone.

'Erasmus laid the egg that the Reformers hatched'

Fisher had chanced to meet Erasmus in London in 1498 when the Dutchman was travelling to Oxford to attend lectures given by John Colet. Colet, a cleric and scholar who had travelled widely in Europe and was something of a 'Renaissance man', became a personal friend of both Erasmus and Thomas More. In fact More studied under Colet before later becoming Henry VIII's Lord Chancellor of England. Colet himself later became Dean of St Paul's Cathedral in London and the founder of St Paul's School. The lectures given by Colet that Erasmus heard in Oxford were on Paul's Epistles and they had a huge influence on him. Earlier Erasmus had studied with the 'Brethren of the Common Life' at Deventer. Then, in 1487 he joined the Augustinian monastery at Steyn near Gouda and was ordained priest five years later. Being on the continent, he assimilated Renaissance ideas well ahead of people in England. He later left the order to study and teach in Paris.

Listening to Colet's lectures, Erasmus resolved to re-read the New Testament in Greek, the original language in which it was written. He already had a thorough knowledge of the Latin version and was a brilliant translator of both Greek and Latin. It was while reading the Greek texts that he realised Jerome's Latin *Vulgate* version contained many errors. He then came to understand that some of the Church's doctrine based on Jerome's erroneous text was also at fault. The Church was at fault morally as many already knew; Erasmus now knew in addition that some of its doctrine was also intellectually corrupt. His publication of the Greek New Testament would reveal this even more clearly.

In his time at Cambridge, Erasmus translated a new Latin version of the New Testament. Named the *Novum Instrumentum* it appeared in manuscript form in 1513 and was read by both Cambridge academics and certain townsfolk. To do this Erasmus

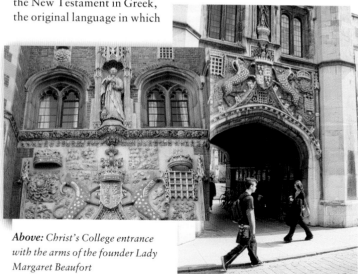

Above: Christ's College entrance with the arms of the founder Lady Margaret Beaufort

Lady Margaret Beaufort

As well as being Bishop of Rochester and Chancellor of Cambridge University, John Fisher had become the private confessor of the mother of King Henry VII, Lady Margaret Beaufort. She too was keen to bring Renaissance ideas to England but Fisher focused her attention on Cambridge, where in 1505 she founded Christ College and, six years later, St John's College. She also established the Lady Margaret Professorship of Divinity at both universities, Oxford and Cambridge. When Fisher invited Erasmus to Cambridge, the latter's travel and college fees were met from Lady Margaret's purse, and he was given lodging in Queens' College where Fisher had been President.

secured from Europe the original Greek source documents never previously seen in England. He displayed the Greek and his own correct Latin in two columns on each page with footnotes as to where the Vulgate had been in error. Erasmus returned to the continent and died in 1535 having always sought to cleanse the Church from within. Inadvertently, he was to have a huge influence on the English Reformers, and Luther also borrowed from him in his own lectures at Wittenberg University.

Top: Lady Margaret Beaufort's statue outside St John's College chapel entrance: raising a model of her new foundation to God for his blessing, she treads not a husband but 'Ignorance' underfoot

Bottom: John Fisher's statue outside St John's College chapel entrance stamping out the evils of simony and church preferment within the church

As the saying goes, 'Erasmus laid the egg that the Reformers hatched'. The combination of Luther and Erasmus would be the catalyst that sparked the Reformation in Cambridge.

John Wycliffe, the 'Morning Star of the Reformation'

Luther drew heavily on the ideas that John Wycliffe, Professor of Theology at Oxford and Master of Balliol College, had voiced in the 14th century. Wycliffe denied papal infallibility as also the Catholic doctrine of transubstantiation. He saw no merit in the many 'medieval superstitious beliefs' promoted by the Church, and saw no reason why people should have to offer prayer via an intermediary, a priest or a monk. He denounced priestly 'auricular' confession, penance and priestly absolution. Sin being an offence against God, he alone can absolve from sin. The Bible, Wycliffe thought, should be in the vernacular, so that those able to read English might benefit from doing so. He himself was largely responsible, directly and indirectly, for the translation of the New Testament into English; he also gave the initial direction to his followers, the Lollards, regarding an Old Testament translation which they duly produced on the continent out of harm's way and then smuggled back into England. Wycliffe's ideas spread to Bohemia and specifically to Jan Hus, Rector of Prague University in the late 14th / early 15th century, before reaching Luther a century later.

Martin Luther

Martin Luther was born in 1483. Having obtained his degree, he became an Augustinian monk and was ordained priest in 1507. A year later he started to lecture at the new University of Wittenberg in Saxony, becoming its Professor of Biblical Exegesis in 1512. By then he had visited Rome where he had been appalled by the corrupt Church practices he discovered—the sale of indulgences in particular. In 1517 he pinned his Ninety-five Theses

Right: St John's College entrance tower with the statue of St John the Evangelist

to the door of the Castle Chapel in Wittenberg; these were short paragraphs attacking the sale of indulgences, an action that led to his excommunication in 1521.

Luther's thinking and actions, however, were no mere reiteration of the pronouncements of Wycliffe and Hus. It was Luther's recapitulation of the views of the apostle Paul and the fifth century theologian Augustine as to how mankind is made righteous before God which spearheaded the Reformation. It is known as 'Justification by Faith'.

Top right: Erasmus' portrait in Queens' College

Right: Martin Luther, the German Reformer

Luther on 'Justification by Faith'

As a young man Luther had never felt reconciled to God. Try as he might, he knew that he always fell short of God's approval and acceptance. Only when he reread the first chapter of Paul's Epistle to the Romans did the light dawn. Verse 17 reads 'He who through faith is righteous will live'. Suddenly the scales fell from his eyes for he now realised that it is not what we do for God but our entire faith in what God has done for us—through Christ's atoning work on the Cross—which is our means of salvation. Made in the image of God, man has fallen too low through sin to be capable of retrieving the situation through his own efforts. Starting from this point, Luther developed his three solas: sola Fide, sola Gratia, sola Scriptura. Faith alone saves; it can not be earned but comes through God's grace, a free gift from God; and we nourish our faith in Scripture not in Church tradition. It therefore follows that as justification before God comes about through 'faith alone' and not through man's 'works', the whole basis of the Catholic penitential system was under threat, since pious acts, prayers and masses cannot of themselves secure the grace of God.

William Tyndale

Following his university student
career at Magdalen Hall,
Oxford, William Tyndale most
likely came to Cambridge some
time before 1520. Tyndale
took lodgings in the town, and
tradition has it that he became a
member of the 'Little Germany'
group which met in the White
Horse Inn near the centre of
town, though this cannot be
verified. In 1523, after two
years as tutor to the children
of Sir John and Lady Walsh
in Gloucestershire, Tyndale
travelled to London in the hope of
gaining permission from Bishop
Tunstall to produce an English
Bible. He was refused. Fleeing to
the continent, his English New
Testament was printed in 1526
and smuggled back into England
just as the Lollards had brought
in their manuscript versions
during the previous century. With
Luther's earlier production of a
German New Testament in 1522,
there was plenty to encourage
Tyndale, though his life was
fraught with danger at every
turn. Luther went on to produce
a complete German translation of
the entire Bible in 1534. Tyndale
had translated fourteen books
of the Old Testament, including
the Pentateuch and the historical
books to 2 Chronicles, before
he was incarcerated in Vilvorde
castle, near Brussels in 1535 and
executed the following year. The
beauty of the English language
owes much to Tyndale. At least
eighty percent of Tyndale's
biblical translation is apparent
in the King James Authorised
Version of 1611. See in this series
Travel with William Tyndale by
Brian Edwards.

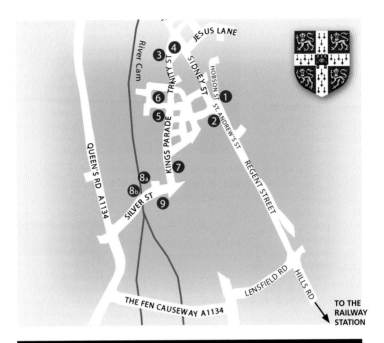

CAMBRIDGE: FROM ITS CENTRE TO THE MILL POND

KEY
1 CHRIST'S COLLEGE
2 ST. ANDREW'S THE GREAT
3 ST. JOHN'S COLLEGE
4 THE 'OLD DIVINITY SCHOOL'
5 THE ORIGINAL DIVINITY SCHOOL
6 GATE OF HONOUR, GONVILLE & CAIUS
7 CORPUS CHRISTI
8A QUEEN'S COLLEGE (SUMMER ENTRANCE)
8B QUEEN'S COLLEGE (WINTER ENTRANCE)
9 THE ANCHOR INN

TRAVEL INFORMATION

Christ's College

St Andrew's Street,
Cambridge, CB2 3BU
www.christs.cam.ac.uk
✆ 01223 334900

Christ's was founded in 1505 by Lady Margaret Beaufort. Alumni include the 16th century Puritan William Perkins, John Milton, William Paley, and Charles Darwin who obtained a theological degree while there. These appear in chapters 4, 5, 6 and 7 respectively. Great St Andrew's Church opposite Christ's College, and often linked with it historically, contains a memorial to Captain James Cook (the naval explorer and ocean surveyor), whose wife and one of six sons are buried there.

The Old Divinity School

St John's Street,
Cambridge

Built in 1879 to replace the original Divinity School (which is still used by the University in a different capacity), its construction was one measure among several taken by J.B. Lightfoot (later bishop) and others to stem secularisation in the University in

Above: *The 'Mathematical Bridge' connecting the older courts of Queens' College with its more modern buildings*

the late 19th century. Its external statues include Matthew Parker (Corpus Christi College and later Archbishop of Canterbury 1559–1575) who saved many priceless manuscripts at the Dissolution of the Monasteries; John Fisher; Erasmus; Thomas Cranmer of Jesus College who later produced the *Book of Common Prayer* and became the first Protestant Archbishop of Canterbury; and Lancelot Andrewes of Pembroke College, the leading Pentateuch translator in preparing the *Authorised Version* of the Bible, and the founder of the 'Caroline Divines' (led by Archbishop Laud), a loose-knit group of spiritual writers who, in the reigns of Charles I and II, helped to promote Anglican ideas.

St John's College

St John's Street,
Cambridge, CB2 1TP
www.joh.cam.ac.uk
✆ 01223 338600

The college stands on the site of the former 'Hospital of St John', run by Augustinians who first administered the Church of the Holy Sepulchre (The Round Church). St John's College, founded by Lady Margaret Beaufort

in 1511 shortly after the hospital's closure, is now the second largest college of the university after Trinity College. It has extensive buildings on both sides of the river linked by two bridges, one being the Bridge of Sighs. Alumni include William Cecil (chapter 4; statue on the chapel exterior), William Wordsworth (chapter 7; features on the chapel vault), William Wilberforce (chapter 7; statue in the ante-chapel) and Lord Palmerston (portrait in the Dining Hall). See also Travel information in chapter seven.

The original Divinity School

Worth a quick viewing from Senate House Passage. Built in the local clunch material (a mix of soft chalk and stone; good for sculpting once the stones are removed but totally inadequate for building purposes), it was completed c.1400. Behind you, as you view it, stands the Gate of Honour of Gonville and Caius, an architectural embellishment inspired by its 16th century Master, John Caius, who refounded the college. Students of the college pass beneath it before collecting their degrees.

Corpus Christi College

Trumpington Street,
Cambridge, CB2 1RH
www.corpus.cam.ac.uk
✆ 01223 338000

Its original court where
Christopher Marlowe
resided as a student is
an eye-opener and the
19th century additions
are worth viewing also.
The (Matthew) Parker
Library can be viewed on
Open Days but requires
special authorisation
from the Librarian. The
original copy of the
'Canterbury Gospels' is
displayed as part of the
collection of manuscripts
saved by Matthew Parker
at the Dissolution of the
Monasteries.

*Left: The plaque to
Christopher Marlowe
and John Fletcher in
Corpus Christi*

*Above: President's
Lodge, Queens' College*

Queens' College

Silver Street, Cambridge,
CB3 9ET
www.queens.cam.ac.uk
✆ 01223 335511

Queens' College was
founded by Margaret
of Anjou, Henry VI's
Queen, in 1448, and is
an attractive college.
Old Court contains
the original college
buildings, the refectory,
library and chapel (since
deconsecrated to become
the student 'Memorial
Library' commemorating
college members who
fell in the Second World
War). The existing college
chapel was built in the
1880s. In Old Court
the famous sun dial
doubles as a moon dial,
and the coat of arms
of the founder denotes
her claims to territory in
many parts of Europe and
Jerusalem! President's
Lodge, a superb half-
timbered building in
Cloister Court is a must
(it is a private residence).
Look for Erasmus' room
at the top of the tower
before crossing the
wooden mathematical
bridge.

The Anchor Inn

Silver Street Bridge,
Cambridge, CB3 9EL
e-mail: 7614@
greeneking.co.uk
✆ 01223 353554

A split-level pub
overlooking the Mill
Pond with punts ready
to take tourists along
the 'Backs'—a part of
Cambridge through which
the river Cam flows and
from which one can see
the backs of many of the
original colleges.

*Above: The interior
of St John's College
chapel, completed 1869
to replace the original
chapel*

❸ 'Little Germany'

Comparison of Luther's early tracts and Erasmus' *Novum Instrumentum* provided the crucible which produced the dynamic for the English Reformation. Cambridge was its cradle, and it was the Reformation which put Cambridge and its university fully on the map

Although Wycliffe died a natural death in 1384, the on-going influence of his followers, the Lollards, left its mark in England throughout the 15th century. This influence came from two sources: partially from those Lollards who escaped to the European mainland and completed their translation of the Old Testament into English before smuggling Bibles back into England; it was also exerted by many Lollards who chose to remain in England, notably in the Thames Valley and Kent and especially in Buckinghamshire and Amersham, where they met in secrecy as house groups in order to promote their ideas. In addition, London merchants sold imported Bibles 'under the counter', whilst in the Hanseatic ports of England and at the London Steelyard there was considerable contact with continental seamen particularly of German and Dutch origin who had themselves been influenced by Protestant ideas circulating on the mainland. The heavy whiff of Wycliffe's influence pervaded Oxford too and it is thought that for this reason, if for no other, Henry VI opted for Cambridge, not Oxford, as a suitable location for his foundation of King's College. The times were ripe in England for the Reformation, which officially started when Martin Luther pinned his '95 Theses' on the chapel door of the castle at Wittenberg, though some of its seeds had been sown earlier.

Above: John Wycliffe in the 'Reformation window' in Trinity College chapel

Facing page: Ridley's walk where he paced up and down whilst committing Paul's Epistles in Greek to memory— seen through the arch in Ivy Court, Pembroke College

Left: The west door of Great St Mary's Church outside which Luther's works were burned in January 1521 though some were saved

In 1520 printed copies of the first three tracts written by Luther found their way into London and Cambridge. Since the Fens, which stretched in a wide arc across the north of Cambridge, were not drained till the 17th century, contraband and radical ideas from the continent could be brought undetected to within a few miles of Cambridge via the many creeks and waterways. Before long however Cardinal Wolsey, Henry VIII's Lord Chancellor, learned of their arrival and ordered their destruction. By May 1521, the bonfires were lit outside the former St Paul's Cathedral in London, with Wolsey present, just a few months after the Cambridge copies had been burned. However, some of the Cambridge copies had been saved in time, and these were given to a group of Cambridge academics and townsfolk such as Robert Barnes, the prior of the

Augustinians in the town centre, who read them carefully and compared them with Erasmus' Novum Instrumentum which had appeared in Cambridge only a few years earlier. The group which came to be known as 'Little Germany'—a pejorative term given it by the citizens of Cambridge once they heard what was happening—found compatibility between Luther and Erasmus. Convinced of the

Above: Thomas Bilney's plaque in Trinity Hall ante-chapel

need to preach the Reformation, the question was: where to do so?

The nominal leader of the 'Little Germany' group was Robert Barnes, a somewhat older man than the others. It was natural therefore that he should 'chair' their meetings on most occasions. Being an Augustinian, Barnes was intensely interested in Luther's pronouncements since Luther himself had been an Augustinian. Indeed Erasmus had also joined the Augustinians earlier in his career, though he later left the order to study and teach in Paris.

Above: *The old Guildhall, Norwich, where the martyr Thomas Bilney was held before being burned in the Lollards' Pit*

'Little Germany'

Apart from Barnes, two of Little Germany's leading lights were Thomas Bilney of Trinity Hall and Hugh Latimer of Clare Hall (now 'College'). Since these colleges lay side-by-side, the two men were well acquainted. It was Bilney, later to become the first leading Protestant martyr in 1531, who converted Latimer and several others to the key Reformation idea of Justification by Faith. Latimer went on to become Bishop of Worcester before suffering martyrdom in the reign of Mary Tudor, together with Ridley at Oxford in October 1555—an

event Cranmer was forced to watch before meeting the same fate five months later. Other members of the group included Nicholas Ridley of Pembroke College, later Bishop of London. William Tyndale, an Oxford student, came to Cambridge before fleeing to the continent where he produced his printed English New Testament and parts of the Old. Miles Coverdale (St Catherine's College) temporarily joined the Augustinians under Robert Barnes, and in 1536 he produced the Coverdale Bible—largely using Tyndale's translations—and three years later the Great Bible; he later fled to the continent in Mary's reign. Others included

John Bradford and John Rogers (who produced the *Matthew's Bible*), both of Pembroke College and both martyred at Smithfield, London. John Frith (King's College and then Cardinal College, Oxford, later renamed Christ Church by Henry VIII), assisted Tyndale with his translations on the continent before returning to England where he was burnt in 1533. As for Matthew Parker (Corpus Christi), he managed to outwit Mary, remaining undetected in East Anglia, before becoming Elizabeth I's Archbishop of Canterbury in 1559. See also in this series *The Martyrs of Mary Tudor* by Andrew Atherstone.

Lesser contributors

Those contributing less significantly, but even so worthy of note, include John Lambert, Rowland Taylor, William Roy and George Joye, (both of whom worked with Tyndale at some time), Nicholas Shaxton (who attained the see of Salisbury through Anne Boleyn's patronage), John Jewel (Bishop of Salisbury under Elizabeth 1), John Bale and Thomas Arthur. It is doubtful whether Thomas Cranmer (Jesus College) was ever a member, though he is known to have preached occasionally at St Edward's where the English Reformers launched their campaign. He was certainly a contemporary and associate of individual members of the group but as a student he was cautious and uncommitted to Luther's ideas apart from which he soon came to the notice of the King.

Surprisingly, on the other hand, there is a suggestion that Stephen Gardiner (Trinity Hall) was a member of the group, though later becoming Bishop of Winchester under Mary; he also became hostile to Cranmer and Protestant ideas in general as well as envious of Reginald Pole, Cranmer's successor as Archbishop. Gardiner became infamous for his inquisition of English Reformers, including Frith.

Site of the White Horse Inn
Known as 'Little Germany' where Cambridge scholars debated the works of Martin Luther in the early sixteenth century
A birthplace of the Reformation in England

Above: The plaque at the southern end of King's Parade which commemorates the site of the White Horse Inn frequented by 'Little Germany'

Top left: A window in Trinity College chapel: William Tyndale is holding his translation of the New Testament

Bottom left: The signboard outside St Edward's King and Martyr with the college arms of Trinity Hall to the left and Clare Hall (now College) on the right

St Edward's Church, a 'royal peculiar'

To understand what happened next in the story that unfolded in Cambridge in the early 1520s we need to go back at least eighty years to a time when neither Trinity Hall nor Clare Hall had serviceable chapels. At that stage, Trinity Hall's chapel was being enlarged and Clare's had been gutted by fire. Both colleges were temporarily using the parish church of St John Zachary. When King Henry VI, the founder of both Eton in 1440 and King's College the following year, realised that he would need to rebuild King's on the site it now occupies, many buildings, including St John Zachary's church were demolished to make way for it. Neither college now had a venue for their worship, whilst the destruction of so much town property meant that the constant hostility between town and gown became even more marked. At that point Simon Dalling, Master of Trinity Hall, approached the king for permission to use another parish church. Henry then authorised the use of St Edward's church which the parish shared thereafter with the two colleges, the three interested parties ensuring that their services didn't clash. The parish continued to use the nave whilst Trinity Hall appropriated the north aisle and Clare the south. Now that the King's permission had been granted to the colleges, St Edward's became what is known in Anglican parlance as a 'royal peculiar' (Latin peculiaris = 'private'), indicating that the crown alone can sanction appointments to its chaplaincy.

The Crown thus became the patron of that church and the local Bishop of Ely no longer had any jurisdiction over what went on inside. He could merely place a cordon of guards outside to act as a deterrent to known frequenters. Once past the guards and inside the church you were safe. Bilney and Latimer were of course members of Trinity Hall and Clare respectively and therefore had automatic access to the building.

Other members of 'Little Germany' also came to have

To the Glory of God
and to honour those from this Parish
who in the years 1523 to 1525
met near by at the White Horse Inn
and there sought out
principles of the English Reformation
THOMAS BILNEY · 1531
ROBERT BARNES · 1540
HUGH LATIMER · 1555
who through faith quenched
the violence of fire.

Above: Inside St Edward's: the plaque commemorating Bilney, Barnes and Latimer and the dates of their execution

access to it in time. Ridley was one of those who preached there, though the leading preachers were Barnes, Bilney and Latimer, and it was Barnes who is considered to have preached the first Reformation sermon there on Christmas Eve 1524. Their earlier sermons attacked the 'medieval superstitious beliefs' that had held sway for so long, but as the English Reformers came to know more about the continental Reformers' thinking, they began to preach the Reformation's key ideas. Other people were then drawn to hear these Reformation sermons, and so the news spread. Before many years had passed other local churches including Great St Mary's were lending support to the cause.

It could be claimed that the start of the English Reformation dates from 1538 when Henry VIII made a radical about-turn and allowed *Matthew's Bible*, compiled by John Rogers, to be 'set forth with the kinges most gracyuous lycense'. Even then however, it remained dangerous to discuss Reformation ideas in public before Henry's death in 1547. Meanwhile Cranmer, who had become Archbishop of Canterbury in 1533, had received Henry's permission to begin the translation of the Mass into English though this only came to completion in the reign of Edward VI. The late 1530s and the early 1540s were years of ongoing tension as Cranmer found to his cost in 1543.

Top: *The wooden pulpit with its linen-fold panelling in St Edward's Church; known as 'Latimer's Pulpit', it was used by the Reformers and by Latimer especially*

Middle: *A window of Emmanuel College chapel—Thomas Cranmer holding his Book of Common Prayer features on the left*

Bottom: *Cranmer's martyrdom at Oxford*

The dissolution of local monasteries

It was Thomas Cromwell who, on behalf of the king, orchestrated the Dissolution of the Monasteries between 1536–1540, thus bringing to an end the large number of Benedictine Abbeys and those of other monastic orders on the islands in the Fens. In Cambridge itself the friar establishments also terminated abruptly, the stone from various monastic buildings being used to help construct a number of colleges. Henry VIII's own foundation of Trinity College (1546) acquired stone from the earlier Franciscan site now occupied by Sidney Sussex College (itself founded in 1596 and benefiting from such stone as Trinity had not used). Emmanuel College (1584) acquired much of the stone of the Dominican establishment previously on their site. Queens' College (1448) absorbed the Carmelite site when it expanded in the following century. Some of the monastic land appropriated elsewhere by the Crown was donated to Trinity College by Henry VIII. This was subsequently let out to tenant farmers and still is, and partially explains the reason for Trinity College's great wealth; it is by far the best endowed of any college in Cambridge or in Oxford.

Above: *Great Court in Trinity College, the largest college court of any Cambridge or Oxford college; it was laid out as it appears at present by its Master, Thomas Nevile, between 1593 and 1615. Later Lord Byron not infrequently bathed at night in the fountain in the centre of the court*

The growing importance of Cambridge University

In the limited number of academic disciplines available for study in the 15th and 16th centuries, most Cambridge students studied theology, and in lesser numbers philosophy, law and medicine. Those subjects apart, there was little else except music and astronomy. Mathematics was only examined for the first time in 1748, some twenty years after Isaac Newton's death, whilst the examination of the classics had to wait until 1824 despite the fact that all lectures for centuries had been given in Latin, with the exception of those in Greek instituted by Erasmus. A greater variety in choice only appeared in the second half of the 19th century.

It is entirely rational that the English Reformation should have first appeared in Cambridge given, first, the proximity of the city to the continent and the ability of small boats to cross the submerged Fenland to within a few miles of Cambridge; second, the fact that some of Luther's works were saved from destruction in Cambridge, and third, the connection of two particular colleges with St Edward's Church. The large number of students reading theology plus the fact that Fellows had without exception to be in holy orders, ensured a fertile breeding ground. Indeed the Reformation put Cambridge on the map theologically and thus academically. This also meant that a university of increasing importance needed a Chancellor elected, not from among the Heads of colleges as had always been the case in the past, but a national figure in the public eye. True, John Fisher had been President of Queens' but he was also Bishop of Rochester and the private confessor of King Henry VII's mother. Fisher was in fact the first Cambridge Chancellor to be elected for life, all previous appointments being limited to a year. These were dangerous times and the new breed of University Chancellors, like any in high office, were frequently in peril as the fortunes of contesting factions fluctuated. Five Chancellors ended their days on the scaffold between Fisher in 1535 and Robert Devereux of Trinity College, later Earl of Essex whom Elizabeth I executed in 1601. Thomas Cromwell, Protector Somerset and the Duke of Northumberland were the other three.

Meanwhile Thomas Lord Audley, successor as Lord Chancellor of England to Sir

Above: *Audley End, the ancient home of the Earls of Suffolk, which stands on the site of the medieval monastery at Walden*

Above: Magdalene College's First Court with shields above the doorways denoting the different Benedictine monasteries whose monks are thought to have inhabited the equivalent premises of the original monks' hospice

Thomas More, had been presented at the Dissolution of the Monasteries with Walden Abbey, near Saffron Walden, south of Cambridge. This came as a reward for services to his king, and in 1542 he founded Magdalene College on the site previously occupied by Buckingham College and before that by a Benedictine monks' hospice. All three in turn stood immediately north of the River Cam on the stretch spanned by the Great Bridge.

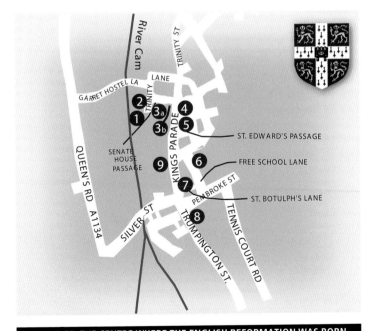

CAMBRIDGE: THE CENTRE WHERE THE ENGLISH REFORMATION WAS BORN

KEY

1 CLARE COLLEGE
2 TRINITY HALL
3A 'OLD SCHOOLS'
3B THE SENATE HOUSE

4 GREAT ST. MARY'S
5 ST. EDWARD'S (KING & MARTYR) CHURCH
6 THE OLD CAVENDISH LABORATORY

7 ST. BOTULPH'S CHURCH
8 PEMBROKE COLLEGE
9 'LITTLE GERMANY' PLAQUE ON WALL

Clare College [ex-'Hall']

Trinity Lane, Cambridge, CB2 1TL
www.clare.cam.ac.uk
✆ 01223 333200

Originally founded as University Hall and refounded in 1338 by Elizabeth de Clare, the college was almost entirely rebuilt in the 17th century after devastation by fire. The Dining Hall houses portraits of Hugh Latimer, Charles ('Turnip') Townsend, the agricultural reformer and the Chancellor of the Exchequer whose policies sparked the Boston Tea-Party and the American War of Independence, and also Charles Cornwallis, the British general

Above: Hugh Latimer's portrait in Clare College

Below: Clare College south facade and Clare bridge

Above: The chancel steps of Great St Mary's with the modern pulpit which can be moved on rails to a central position for University Sermons

Below: The north range of 'Old Schools', the first of the University's buildings to be built (1350–1400 AD), though subsequent to the completion of several colleges, of which Peterhouse was the first (1284)

who lost the Battle of Yorktown. Nicholas Ferrar, the founder of the Little Gidding community which inspired verse from T.S. Eliot, was also an alumnus.

Trinity Hall

Trinity Lane, Cambridge, CB2 1TJ
www.trinhall.cam.ac.uk
✆ 01223 332500

It was founded in 1350 by Bishop Bateman of Norwich primarily for lawyers and some theologians, so many of the latter dying in the Black Death as a result of attending others in extremis. Bateman was a diplomat at the Pope's court in Avignon, and he wished to improve the canon law expertise among the English diplomats attending it. The ante-chapel contains Thomas Bilney's plaque. In recent years Robert Runcie was Dean of this college before becoming Archbishop of Canterbury.

Next proceed up Senate House Passage. Before reaching the Senate House, the hub of the University and the building in which degrees are conferred, look right to a medieval building half hidden by a facade. This is known as 'Old Schools' and is now used for administrative purposes; formerly it housed the Divinity School where Erasmus taught.

Great St Mary's Church

St Mary's Passage,
Cambridge, CB2 3PQ
www.gsm.cam.ac.uk
✆ 01223 741716

The church is open daily unless a special service is being conducted there. It is the central Anglican church in town, but also the University church. It was used for degree ceremonies before the Senate House was completed. In very early times examinations were held here in the form of oral disputation. Examiner and student sat opposite each other on three-legged ('tripod') stools, hence the term 'Tripos' denoting modern Cambridge examinations. Fires have often featured in this church's history. In 1290 the previous church was gutted. In 1381 a mob sympathetic to the Peasants' Revolt broke in and seized the University's archives and papers, burning these in the Market Square. Luther's books were burnt outside the west door in January 1521 though some were saved. Oliver Cromwell is also alleged to have entered during a service, and finding the Book of Common Prayer in use instead of the prescribed Presbyterian Directory, he ripped apart a copy of the former before setting it alight.

St Edward's Church

St Edward's Passage, Peas Hill, Cambridge, CB2 3PP
www.st-edwards-cam.org.uk
✆ 01223 362004

The church is generally open on Wednesdays and Fridays 1300–1500 hrs as staffing permits. This is where the early Reformers first preached. Though now a parish church again, it still comes under Trinity Hall's patronage. The stained glass commemorates Bilney and Latimer as also Simon Dalling, Master of Trinity Hall, who obtained Henry VI's permission for its use by his college and by Clare. Edward Lively (Clare College) and Richard Thompson (Corpus Christi), two of the translators of the 1611 Authorised Version of the Bible, feature on a plaque as does the 19th century Christian Socialist F.D. Maurice on another. Yet another plaque

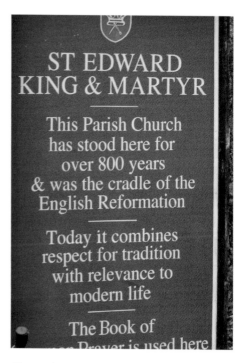

Above: The sign in St Edward's Passage indicating the start point of the English Reformation

commemorates Bilney, Barnes and Latimer.

At the southern end of King's Parade opposite the turning into Bene't Street, a blue plaque on the wall to your right commemorates the White Horse Inn where the Reformers met. Turn up Bene't Street, turn right again and you are in Free School Lane. The buildings on your left mark the site of the Augustinian religious house where Barnes was Prior. Continue past the Old Cavendish Laboratory buildings on your left. Near the end of the lane take the first turning right, i.e. Botolph Lane, passing St Botolph's Church. St Botolph was patron saint of travellers in East England. Turn left and cross Pembroke Street. Pembroke College is now on your left.

Pembroke College

Trumpington Street, Cambridge, CB2 1RF
www.pem.cam.ac.uk
✆ 01223 338100

The third oldest existing Cambridge college, it was founded in 1347 by a French lady, the widow of the Earl of Pembroke, who wished to improve Anglo-French relations during the Hundred Years' War. Its early statutes allowed French students to be educated alongside English. Famous alumni include Nicholas Ridley, Edmund Spenser (chapter 4), Thomas Gray (chapter 6) and William Pitt the Younger (chapter 6). Its chapel is the very first of Christopher Wren's buildings to be completed (1665).

Above: William Pitt the Younger's statue outside Pembroke College library; Pitt was Britain's youngest ever Prime Minister and held office from 1783 until his death in 1806, with one short break

4 A Puritan hot-house

By attacking the supremacy of the Roman Catholic Church, the Reformation sowed the seeds of its internal divisions. Many Puritans demanded a 'purer' reform than the compromise which the emerging Church of England represented. This was particularly apparent at Cambridge

The English Reformation was another chapter in the long running dispute over the claim of the papacy to control the lives of English people. At the outset it was more of a political than a theological dispute, since Henry's determination to divorce Catherine of Aragon and marry Anne Boleyn drove him further away from papal domination. The king's separation of the Church of England from Rome began in 1529 and was completed by 1536, but the structure and theology of that Church in England was a matter of fierce dispute for generations, not least in Cambridge.

Having been the cradle of the English Reformation, Cambridge became, in the later 16th century, increasingly the battleground for ideas ranging from conservative Anglicanism to more extreme Puritanism; it therefore had an important role to play on the national and international stage. Puritan foundations were established at two colleges: Emmanuel, by Sir Walter Mildmay (Elizabeth I's Chancellor and brother-in-law of Sir Francis Walsingham, the spy-master, who had himself been at King's College), and Sidney Sussex, by Lady Frances Sidney, Countess of Sussex, the aunt of the poet Sir Philip Sidney.

Earlier however, Thomas Cranmer, a student and Fellow of Jesus College, Cambridge, broke his priestly vows by marrying 'Black Joan', daughter of the proprietor of the Dolphin Inn, Cambridge, which required him to relinquish his Fellowship. Joan died a year later in child-birth, and Cranmer, who had meanwhile become a humble lecturer at Magdalene College, was able to renew his Fellowship at Jesus College. Cranmer came to Henry's notice in 1529, when he suggested that the King ask the scholars of the universities of Christendom, especially those of Oxford and Cambridge, for a solution to his 'Great Matter' (the divorce of Catherine), which they indeed obligingly produced in favour of the king. In 1533 Cranmer was consecrated Archbishop of

Facing page: Looking towards the chancel steps in Great St Mary's, where John Whitgift abruptly terminated Thomas Cartwright's teaching in Cambridge, and where Oliver Cromwell in fury ripped apart a Book of Common Prayer

Canterbury, taking the oath of allegiance to the pope 'for form's sake'. He then immediately pronounced Catherine's marriage null and void, whilst validating the private marriage of Anne Boleyn to Henry, which had occurred four months earlier.

In 1536 the Dissolution of the Monasteries got under way, orchestrated by Thomas Cromwell who became Chancellor of Cambridge University; it was partly motivated by Henry's extravagant life-style and his consequent insatiable greed for wealth. The sale of monastic lands swelled the Crown's coffers handsomely, but it also had the effect of sealing off one of the last remaining channels of papal influence in England. As for the monastic art and literary treasures awaiting looters and vandals, reference has already been made (see page 12) to the actions of Matthew Parker of Corpus Christi who saved so many priceless treasures.

Above: *Prior Crauden's chapel and buildings remaining from the abbey at Ely; some of the less damaged were appropriated by King's School, Ely, one of the oldest schools in England*

Bottom: *Thomas Cranmer's statue on the new (now 'Old') Divinity School*

Cranmer, who has often been blamed for a failure to oppose the king more vigorously, was an 'Erastian'. Erastianism is the belief, based on Paul's words in Romans 13, that all people should be subject to the governing authorities. A ruler's harsh treatment of his subjects was therefore taken to be God's means of chastising a people in error. Cranmer thus survived the turbulent controversies with the hard-line conservative bishops of the early 1540s, at which time Henry allowed him to start translating the liturgy into English, although it was only in Edward VI's reign that this task was completed. In 1549 Cranmer produced his first version of the *Book of Common Prayer*; the second version appeared in 1552, and was considerably more Protestant in tone. To assist him with the latter, Cranmer enlisted the aid of Martin Bucer, having first invited the German from Strasburg to become Regius Professor of Theology at Cambridge. Bucer died in 1551, but in 1557 he was deemed a heretic, and his body exhumed on Mary Tudor's orders and burned in the Market Square together with another German Paul Fagius, Professor of Hebrew, who had died in 1549. The only Cambridge Protestant to be burned alive by Mary in Cambridge—on Jesus Green, where a plaque records the event of 1556—was John Hullier, chaplain of King's College.

Top: Martin Bucer's mortuary plaque on the sanctuary floor in Great St Mary's, showing the dates of his death (1551), his exhumation under Mary in 1557, and his rehabilitation and reburial under Elizabeth I in 1560

Bottom: The corpses of Martin Bucer and Paul Fagius being burned in their coffins on 'Market Hill'. From Foxe's 'Book of Martyrs'

Above: The wooden bench on Jesus Green with the plaque recording John Hullier's martyrdom

her reign, ran the constant risk of imprisonment, torture and death at the stake. John Foxe in his Book of Martyrs lists some 283 such men and women. Latimer, Ridley and Cranmer were all burned at the stake in Broad Street, Oxford, only a short distance from where the Martyrs' Memorial was later erected to commemorate them. Hence the saying 'What Cambridge grew, Oxford slew'. Others such as Rogers and Bradford died at Smithfield, London; Frith had met the same fate there in 1533 under Henry VIII.

'Visitations' to the college libraries

During Mary's reign, Cardinal Pole, who became Archbishop of Canterbury following Cranmer's execution, paid an official visit to all Cambridge libraries to root out Protestant works. An equivalent 'visitation' had occurred in Edward VI's reign, its target being popish literature. As a direct result of both visitations, the libraries and book stores of Cambridge and its colleges were thoroughly depleted with little left to study! Potential students were also wary of inadvertently associating with groups of academics who might later be branded reactionary or heretic. For both reasons student numbers at Cambridge declined dramatically for over a decade in the late 1540s.

Elizabeth I

Elizabeth and her advisors disliked the popular aspects of the Presbyterian form of church government, favouring instead

The Counter Reformation

In the meantime Chancellors of Cambridge University came and went, the Dukes of Somerset and Northumberland falling from power in quick succession and ending their days on the scaffold as Edward VI's reign closed and Mary succeeded to the throne—an event marking the start of the Counter Reformation in this country. In continental Europe, the Counter Reformation began at the Council of Trent (1545–1563) in a vigorous attempt by the Roman Catholic Church to claw back ground lost to the Protestants. With Mary on the throne, supported by bishops such as Stephen Gardiner who became Bishop of Winchester (there is a portrait of him in Trinity Hall Dining Room), many Protestants fled to Holland and the Rhineland where they remained until Mary's death in 1558. Those leading Protestants who remained in England during

Left: Trinity Hall Old Library (completed 1598) with many of its original book cases

The Elizabethan Settlement

When Mary died, the English Protestants who had fled to the continent returned, believing they would be able to celebrate, without fear of persecution, the 'pure' form of worship they craved. Instead, they found themselves increasingly forced to comply with the Anglican Church's emerging stipulations. The Elizabethan Religious Settlement was Queen Elizabeth's response to the religious divisions created in the reigns of Henry VIII, Edward VI and Mary. This response was set out in two acts of Parliament. The 1559 Act of Supremacy re-established the church's independence from Rome, with Parliament conferring on Elizabeth the secular title 'Supreme Governor of the Church of England', avoiding the pitfalls created by Henry's 'Supreme Head …'; this was a theological title which had so outraged Thomas More and John Fisher, since St Paul's Epistles state unequivocally that Christ alone is the Head of the church. That same year the Act of Uniformity was passed. This set out the form the English Church would now take, and re-established the Book of Common Prayer, albeit marginally revised.

Eventually in 1613 Dissenters (those who dissented from the Anglican form of worship) were denied the right to graduate at Cambridge. Back in 1563 Convocation passed the Thirty-nine Articles of Religion, which are the tenets of faith setting out the Anglican doctrinal position. The Settlement is often seen as a terminal point for the English Reformation. Viewed retrospectively, the Anglican Church adopted a compromise, but at the time it was thought to have established a Protestant Church, one among other Protestant Churches in Europe. It was, however, to provoke great divisions within the country's population and among its clergy.

an Episcopal organisation (government of the church by bishops) that left the ultimate authority over the church in the hands of civil authorities. She cared little that an altar had no saint's relics buried beneath it; neither was a church's east-facing orientation of concern to her; if, as at Sidney Sussex, an altar faced was thankfully destroyed by the storms off England's coasts in 1588. England itself came to be seen by Englishmen as God's 'Promised Land', a Canaan to the Israelites, and the English finally believed they were God's chosen people, hedged in by the Catholic forces of darkness. In contrast, those ministers within the Church

of England with Puritan aspirations found themselves increasingly obliged to toe the line or leave the church, and in cases of threatened persecution to flee to Holland or the Rhineland yet again.

south, so be it. Nor had she any wish to 'make windows into men's souls'. The crucial matter was the form of church government, and she therefore made it clear from the start, that despite being Protestant, she had little liking for the more extreme reformers who considered her a compromiser. In any case, particularly after her excommunication by the Pope in 1570, Elizabeth could ill afford a divided nation whose population, barely four million and a quarter of that of France, was still mainly Catholic. The might of France, with Scotland in alliance, was second only to that of Spain—whose Armada

Priestly celibacy

Priests had been allowed to marry in Edward VI's reign only to be forced to leave their wives when Mary came to the throne; they were now allowed to marry again, though not the Fellows of Oxford and Cambridge; Fellows at Cambridge were only released from this obligation in 1882. Elizabeth I believed that the future leaders of England would come invariably from Oxford and Cambridge, the only universities in her realm, and this proved to be the case with few exceptions prior to the 18th century. Her view was that if they had family matters to attend to, they would fail to concentrate entirely on the students in their care. The reward for this major sacrifice was that they and they alone had exclusive permission to walk on the lawns of their own colleges! Unable to marry and have families, colleges became 'home' to the Fellows, who at their death bequeathed considerable legacies to them.

Above: Roger Ascham's statue on St John's College chapel

Left: Sidney Sussex College chapel which has its altar facing south

The Elizabethan 'Golden Age'

Elizabeth's reign has been called the 'Golden Age', and Cambridge was no exception. As a girl, Elizabeth had been tutored by Roger Ascham, whose statue is on the outer wall of St John's College chapel; Ascham later became Latin secretary to Queen Mary, whilst John Cheke, also of St John's and the first Regius Professor of Greek at Cambridge and Provost of King's College, had tutored the young Prince of Wales (later Edward VI). The early writings of the poet Edmund Spenser, author of 'The Faerie Queene', were penned whilst still a student at Pembroke College. Christopher Marlowe of Corpus Christi College often forsook his studies to act in plays performed in the courtyard of the Eagle Inn nearby. Thomas Gresham of Gonville and Caius College became Lord Mayor of London and later Elizabeth I's ambassador to the Netherlands; he also founded both the Royal Exchange and Gresham's College in London.

The scientist William Gilbert (St John's College) produced his work on magnetism, *De Magnete*, in 1600. William Cecil (the later Lord Burghley) also at St John's, became Chancellor of the University, was appointed Chief Secretary of State in 1558, and for the next forty years was the chief architect of the successful policies of the Elizabethan era and involved in the Queen's state visit to Cambridge in 1564. Interestingly Cecil was himself married to a Puritan, Mildred Cook, daughter of a Puritan father who had to flee the country. Robert Devereux

(Trinity College), became Earl of Essex and University Chancellor before overreaching himself; Elizabeth no longer viewed him as her 'favourite' but as powerful enough to pose a threat to her own position and for this he was executed in 1601. As for the Archbishops of Canterbury in Elizabeth's reign and beyond, the list of Cambridge alumni is impressive and continuous, beginning with Matthew Parker (Corpus Christi) in 1559, the year of the Queen's accession, followed by Edmund Grindal (Pembroke College), John Whitgift (Trinity College), and in 1604 Richard Bancroft (Trinity Hall). Edwin Sandys (St John's College) became Archbishop of York.

Cambridge Puritans

The history of Cambridge in the later 16th century was above all one of theological controversy.

As the Anglican Church began to define itself more clearly, so Cambridge dissidents voiced their objections increasingly. Thomas Cartwright, the 'Father of English Presbyterianism' and a Fellow of Trinity College, railed against the vestments and hierarchical structure of the church, finding nothing in the Book of Acts to support them. He was stripped of his Fellowship and Professorship of Divinity by

Above: The statue of William Cecil, Lord Burghley, on a St John's chapel wall

Right: The French Renaissance facade of the 19th century extension of Gonville and Caius College, where Thomas Gresham was a student. The statues are: Gonville, the founder (below), Bishop Bateman of Norwich (top right) and John Caius who refounded the college (top left)

Left: *William Gilbert's plaque outside St John's College where he studied*

Below: *Laurence Chaderton (right), the first Master of Emmanuel College, alongside John Harvard in an Emmanuel College chapel window*

John Whitgift, his Master of College, who later became Vice-Chancellor of Cambridge University in a career which led to the Archbishopric of Canterbury. As for new Cambridge colleges, two Puritan foundations were established in 1584 (Emmanuel) and 1596 (Sidney Sussex).

Above:
St Andrew's the Great, where William Perkins held his 'prophesying' sessions

William Perkins and 'prophesying'

William Perkins of Christ's College and 'lecturer' at St Andrew's Church across the road, was a noted preacher and pastor, influencing many students who later became Puritan leaders. Among the best known was William Ames, also of Christ's College and one of several Cambridge academics to attend the Synod of Dort in 1618 which refuted the 'free-will' doctrine of the Dutchman, Jacobus Arminius and opposed it with Calvin's doctrine of 'predestination' wholly or in part; this controversy resurfaced later as the 'Arminian Debate'. Before his conversion, Perkins was often the worse for drink. One day, passing a woman in a Cambridge street, he heard her say to her child: 'There goes that drunkard Perkins'. He was so ashamed, that this led to a total change in his life. Among his writings, Perkins produced substantial treatises, e.g. De Praedestinatione ('On Predestination') which provoked the Dutch theologian Arminius to reply. Perkins was a prolific commentator on Scripture and a formidable scholar. His writing on preaching and the role of the ministry had considerable influence both at home and abroad.

Though associated with the Presbyterian movement, he never publicly advocated a Presbyterian system of church government. Perkins was a leader among those who assembled in local churches to hold mid-week 'prophesyings' (given by 'endowed' lecturers), where a minister would offer expository teaching of biblical texts and afterwards, those attending, including ministers and laity as well as the usual Sunday congregation, were invited to discuss what they had heard. Perkins was the author of The Art of Prophesying, one of the first books to be written on preaching.

Other leading Cambridge Puritans included Robert Browne of Corpus Christi who became disaffected with Cartwright's teaching and developed his own brand of Puritan Separatism. In 1579 he started preaching in Cambridgeshire churches, refusing to accept the Bishop's permission to officiate, on the grounds that the calling and authority of bishops was unlawful and that true authority lay in the 'gathered' church. Browne organised separatist churches locally, effectively undermining the church-state relationship achieved by the Elizabethan Settlement. Persecuted by the authorities and imprisoned, he owed his release to his relationship with Lord Burghley; in 1582 he and his new Church settled in Holland. By 1585 Browne had made peace with Archbishop Whitgift and six years later was sufficiently orthodox to be ordained to a Northampton living. Those Separatists who felt let down by him, came to hold him in considerable contempt, including Henry Barrow (Clare College) and John Greenwood (Corpus Christi), who were hung for sedition in London in 1592. Browne's earlier Separatist followers were later known as Brownists; they in turn became the Congregationalists.

John Smyth was at Corpus Christi before becoming a Fellow of Christ's College. In 1600, shortly after ordination, Smyth became 'lecturer' at Lincoln Cathedral. Dismissed two years later for 'personal preaching', he became pastor of a Brownist congregation at Gainsborough, before fleeing in 1607 with its members to Holland to escape persecution. Convinced of the necessity of 'believers' baptism' (adult baptism), he became known as the 'Father of the English Baptists'. Smyth further believed that all praying, singing and preaching should be completely spontaneous. Nor was the reading of the Bible in worship permissible, since he regarded English translations as something less than the word of God.

Later, Richard Sibbes and Thomas Goodwin continued to head the Puritan concentration in Cambridge. Thomas Goodwin from Christ's College resigned as vicar of Holy Trinity on becoming a Congregationalist. Leaving for London and abroad, he then returned to enjoy the confidence of Oliver Cromwell and was one of the Dissenting members of the Westminster Assembly. Goodwin became Warden of Magdalen College, Oxford, and a prominent member of the Savoy Assembly of Congregational elders in 1658. By then, however, the High Anglicanism of Charles I had caused others to emigrate to New England, but that is a subject for the chapter which follows.

Far left: William Perkins' portrait held by St Andrew's the Great

Left: Henry Barrow and John Greenwood in an Emmanuel U.R.C. window

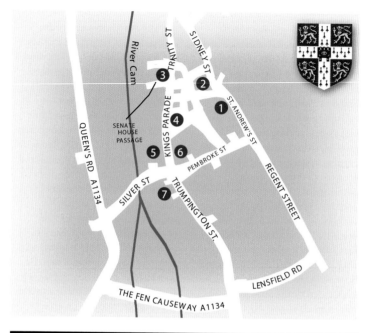

CAMBRIDGE: PURITAN ESTABLISHMENTS

KEY

1 ST. ANDREW'S THE GREAT
2 HOLY TRINITY CHURCH
3 GONVILLE AND CAIUS COLLEGE
4 THE EAGLE INN
5 ST. CATHERINE'S COLLEGE
6 CORPUS CHRISTI COLLEGE
7 EMMANUEL UNITED REFORMED CHURCH

Above: St Andrew's the Great in the 18th century

TRAVEL INFORMATION

St Andrew's the Great Church

St Andrew's Street,
Cambridge, CB2 3AX
www.stag.org
✆ 01223 518218

Entry by intercom at the door. Traditionally linked with Christ's College opposite, this is the church where William Perkins held 'prophesying' sessions, exerting great influence on so many who became Puritans in their turn. It is now a traditional stronghold of modern evangelical students.

Holy Trinity Church

Market Street, Cambridge,
CB2 3NZ
www.htcambridge.org.uk
✆ 01223 355397

Entry via intercom at the door. This was Thomas Goodwin's church, and later that of Charles Simeon (chapter 6) whose influence was felt so widely. His plaque is mounted on the inner south chancel wall.

Gonville and Caius College

Trinity Street, Cambridge,
CB2 1TA
www.cai.cam.ac.uk
✆ 01223 332400

Founded in 1348 by Gonville, a Norfolk priest, and refounded in the 16th century by John Caius, Royal Physician to the City of London, who is buried in the chapel. This was Thomas Gresham's college (see page 57). It has also had a remarkable medical tradition, including William Harvey (chapter 6), private physician to Charles I, later Warden of Merton College, Oxford, and notable for our understanding of blood circulation and embryology. Other outstanding physicians from this college include Francis Glisson (the 'Glisson glove' surrounds the liver); Robert Brady (re-introduced quinine, abandoned in 16th/17th century Protestant England, being an extraction from cinchona bark, alias 'Jesuit's bark', with an unfortunate Catholic association!); and William Wollaston (produced pure platinum, and isolated two new elements, palladium and rhodium).

Above:
The south west corner of the chapel in Caius Court, Gonville and Caius College

'The Eagle'

8. Bene't Street,
Cambridge, CB2 3QN
email: 3004@greeneking.
co.uk
✆ 01223 505020

With history dating from the 16th century, this former tavern is associated with Marlowe and the plays performed in its courtyard. Pictures inside the inn attest to personalities who have been its clients. Wilberforce (chapter 7) for example idled his student time away playing cards here, whilst in World War II airmen from the RAF and the American 8th and 9th Air Forces, when off duty, drank and inscribed their names on the ceiling of

Top: The front facade of Gonville and Caius with the first floor figurines

Bottom: Thomas Gresham's statue opposite the front facade of Gonville and Caius

Right: The original court in Corpus Christi College where Christopher Marlowe was a student

one particular bar. The air crew of the famous 'Memphis Belle', the B17 American bomber, are commemorated in one of the many photos on its walls. Warm food awaits at luncheon.

St Catherine's College

Trumpington Street, Cambridge, CB2 1RL
www.caths.cam.ac.uk
✆ 01223 338300

Founded in 1473 and built in the local soft clunch material, this college had to be entirely rebuilt two centuries later. Miles Coverdale, who was responsible for the Great Bible, was a student here. Later, one of its Masters was Richard Sibbes, a leading Puritan in Cambridge. The college commemorates St Catherine, an early 4th century martyr under the Roman Emperor Maxentius.

Corpus Christi College

King's Parade, Cambridge, CB2 1RH
www.corpus.cam.ac.uk
✆ 01223 338000

Founded by two town guilds in 1352 as a 'chantry college', the Master and Fellows' first priority was to pray for the souls of those many townsfolk taken by the Black Death four years earlier. This was Marlowe's college, as also that of Matthew Parker, Robert Browne, John Smyth (all mentioned in this chapter) and John Robinson (chapter 5). The original court is one of the very earliest in Cambridge. It's 19th century chapel and New Court were added by the architect William Wilkins who designed the National Gallery.

Emmanuel United Reformed Church

Little St Mary's Lane, Cambridge,
www.emmanuelurc. org.uk
✆ 01223 351174

Open late morning and offering a light lunch menu, it is a spacious late 19th century church with stained glass commemorating, among other Puritans, Henry Barrow and John Greenwood (both mentioned above).

Top: *The courtyard of the 'Eagle Inn' where plays were performed in the 16th century*

⑤ Civil War and New England emigrants

The tensions brewing in the 16th century continued into the 17th with the High Anglicanism of the King and his Archbishop; they encouraged a mass emigration to New England and a bloody Civil War in England

The religious divide between the Anglican Church and those Puritans seeking a 'pure' and therefore complete Reformation, continued into the 17th century. With the accession of James I in 1603, there was a renewed attempt by Puritans desiring a Presbyterian style of church organisation and worship to press their case. They presented the King with the Millenary Petition signed by some 1,000 petitioners, requesting an open debate on the issue. This led to the Hampton Court Conference of 1604 at which the eager Presbyterians (led by Lawrence Chaderton, the first Master of Emmanuel College which, ever since its 1584 foundation, had been a Puritan establishment), gained precisely nothing from the Anglicans present, except agreement to produce a new version of the Bible. This was the *Authorised Version* which appeared in 1611; its translators were convened from Cambridge (see page 68), Oxford and the Cambridge dominated government. The degree of hostility that Chaderton and his team experienced at Hampton was to some extent ironic, since the leading Anglican present was none other than Richard Bancroft, now Archbishop of Canterbury, but formerly of Trinity Hall and an earlier friend of Chaderton. The latter, a man of huge physique and athletic prowess, had once saved Bancroft from a lynching by a Cambridge mob. Chaderton was a prolific preacher; one sermon he gave in Great St Mary's lasted three hours—not uncommon after the Reformation when the focus in services swung away from the liturgy and altar on to readings from Scripture and the sermon.

Facing page: *Sir Peter Lely's portrait of Oliver Cromwell*

Above: *Archbishop Laud's portrait by van Dyck. Laud presented it to the Trinity Hall Master, Thomas Eden (Sir Anthony Eden's ancestor), one of the few supporters of Laud's right of visitation to Cambridge University (which never occurred). The portrait hangs in the College Dining Hall*

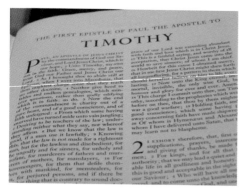

Left: The Authorised Version of the Bible in St Edward's, open at the first chapter of Paul's First Epistle to Timothy; verse 15 brought Thomas Bilney to an understanding of 'Justification by Faith'

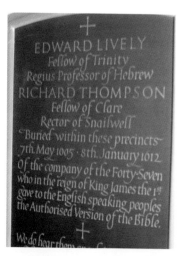

Matthew Wren and High-Anglicanism

James I was succeeded by Charles I in 1625. It was not only the high-handedness of Charles I and his questionable morality—siphoning off taxes such as 'Ship Tax' to line his own pocket—which turned many against him, but also his leading of the church in a direction about which many felt unhappy. The High Anglicanism of Charles I and Archbishop William Laud reintroduced much of the symbolism lost at the Reformation. Laud's threatened visitation to Cambridge never materialised, partly because it was boycotted by many college Heads, though some in anticipation took steps to comply by raising altars in their chapels.

Top left: The plaque in the church of St Edward displaying the names of two of the Cambridge translators of the Authorised Version, Edward Lively and Richard Thompson

Left: The east window of Pembroke College chapel where Matthew Wren, holding a model of his chapel, kneels at the foot of the Cross. To the left of the Cross kneels the college founder

Elsewhere those Puritans seeking greater freedom in worship began to emigrate to New England. One of the associates of King Charles and Archbishop Laud was Matthew Wren (uncle of the great architect Christopher Wren), who after his time at Pembroke College became Master of Peterhouse, and eventually Bishop of Ely. Laud and Thomas Wentworth (Earl of Strafford and formerly at St John's College) were later impeached by John Pym, the leader of the Puritans in the Long Parliament, and imprisoned in the Tower of London prior to their executions (Strafford in 1641, Laud in 1645). Wren, however, emerged after eighteen years of imprisonment and in gratitude to God for his deliverance he requested his nephew to design a new chapel to God's glory at Pembroke, which he held in particular affection. The chapel's design is based on the theme of death and new life, recalling Christ's crucifixion and resurrection, the execution of Charles I in 1649 and the monarchy's restoration in 1660, and his own living death in the Tower followed by his release. Matthew Wren is buried in the crypt beneath this chapel.

Dutch navvies in the Fens

In the 17th century Cornelius Vermuyden and his Dutch navvies, who had experience of land reclamation in Holland, were invited by the Duke of Bedford to drain the Fens (see also page 7), much of which he owned. It had been partially but unsuccessfully attempted by the Romans and the Normans, but the Dutchmen were masters of their science. They dug the Old and New Bedford Rivers in 1631 and 1651 respectively, and the giant Denver sluice north-east of Ely was then built to control

Above: The Bible cushions, displaying the three crowns of Ely Diocese, given by Matthew Wren on Pembroke chapel's dedication in 1665, the first of his nephew's (Christopher Wren) buildings to be completed

New England and North American history

The leaders of those who emigrated to New England between 1628 and 1640 were well educated. Oxford and Cambridge still remained the only two universities in the land, and of the first 132 graduates to arrive in New England, 100 came from Cambridge, and of those, 35 from Emmanuel College. Earlier, the Pilgrim Fathers, whose chaplain John Robinson (Corpus Christi) remained in Holland to tend the remnant of his flock, had made the Atlantic crossing in 1620. Among those who had sailed on the Mayflower was William Brewster (Peterhouse) who became the 'elder' and leader of the Plymouth Colony settlement. Other early leaders included John Winthrop (Trinity College), who became Governor of Massachusetts in 1630; so too John Cotton ('The Patriarch of Boston'), Nathaniel Ward ('The Law-Giver') and John Harvard (who, at his death in 1638, left his library and half his estate to help a college that became what is now Harvard University). The latter three had all been to Emmanuel College. The majority of the Emmanuel men were committed Puritans and evangelical Christians. On arrival, the colonists were received amicably by the natives, and it was only later that trouble arose with the 'Redskins'. The immediate problem, however, was the language barrier. In response to a request for a linguist, John Eliot (Jesus College), a minister near Hertford, England, volunteered to join the settlers. Living among the natives he learned first to speak Algonquin, then to master the written language. In 1661 he began translating the Bible, a task he completed two years later. It was the second book and the first Bible to be produced in North America, and Jesus College Old Library holds an original copy.

Left: *The original court of Emmanuel College, with its earlier chapel (left) and Dining Hall (right). Previously, the Dominicans had used both buildings, but with their functions reversed*

inland flooding by holding back the sea. A century later some 750 wind-pumps were installed to help expel the water, but they were of no avail on a windless day. This function was replaced around 150 years later by large electrically driven pumps. Were they all to stop simultaneously, Cambridge scientists calculate that the waters would reclaim the land and be at Cambridge's back door within six months!

Among the townsfolk, Thomas Hobson was a considerable benefactor to both town and colleges alike. Besides being the owner of stables (see page 11), it was Hobson who in 1614 was chiefly responsible for introducing drinking water to Cambridge. Fed from springs to the south, the water reached Cambridge via a purpose-built conduit, which then branched into two gutters running along Trumpington Street, before continuing underground to fountains installed in colleges and the market square. Previously everyone drank small ale (watered-down beer), the alcohol content hopefully killing off the bacteria in the water. At St John's the student ration had been eight pints per day; they had been allowed to imbibe even at breakfast.

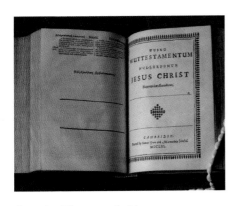

Opposite: The west end of the Christopher Wren chapel at Emmanuel College, whose exterior was completed in 1673; it is more baroque in style than the classical facade of the west end of Pembroke College chapel, completed by Wren in 1665

Above: *The Algonquin Bible in Jesus College old library*

Left: Cornelius Vermuyden who drained the Fens in the 17th century

Below: The Fens in Cambridgeshire and Lincolnshire

As for the academics, a group called the 'Cambridge Platonists' (pejoratively known as 'latititudinarians') sought to synthesise Greek Philosophy and Christian theology. The Platonists, many of whom were members of Emmanuel College, were led by Benjamin Whichcote. Several were installed by the Parliamentarians as Master or Senior Fellow in colleges with Royalist sympathies, Whichcote becoming Provost of King's. Many of them were later ousted from their new posts at the Restoration of the Monarchy. Shortly after, (at the 1662 Savoy Conference, when the Prayer Book was re-introduced) the Presbyterians again failed to make headway against the Anglican Church. This led to the huge number of 2000 church ministers being ejected from their positions, including some of the Platonists. In turn, this produced a fresh wave of New England emigrants, many of whom had an intense dislike of the very liberal and licentious society that emerged under Charles II and his lackeys. Furthermore, Charles' earlier promise of amnesty to all, except for the fifty-nine signatories of his father's death warrant, was soon forgotten and persecution of 'non-conformists' began.

Civil War and its aftermath

In the Middle Ages a group of Benedictine nuns decided to move from their marshy surroundings in Eltisley, west of Cambridge, to higher, drier ground at Hinchingbrooke, near Huntingdon. At the Dissolution of the Monasteries, this establishment was closed by Thomas Cromwell and the property given to his nephew, Richard, who at his death bequeathed it to his son, Sir Henry Cromwell; the latter entertained Elizabeth I lavishly on her 1564 Cambridge visit, and later James VI of Scotland as he headed south to accept the crown of England. Both monarchs brought huge courts, and supporting these and other

Right: Hobson's conduit and fountain; the latter, previously in the Market Square, was later moved to its current site on the corner of Lensfield Road opposite the Royal Cambridge Hotel

Bottom left: Hobson's conduit, in Trumpington Street where it splits into two gutters on each side of the street

Other Cambridge alumni

Some Cambridge students became great poets, including Robert Herrick (Trinity Hall), author of 'Cherry Ripe', and 'Gather ye rosebuds while ye may'; deprived of his living in Devon for being a Royalist, he resumed it after the Restoration. Trinity College produced 'metaphysical' poets, including John Donne (later Dean of St Paul's Cathedral, London), Andrew Marvel (tutor to Lord Fairfax's daughter and also to a ward of Oliver Cromwell), who later became John Milton's assistant, and George Herbert (later a 'Caroline Divine', as was Lancelot Andrewes (see page 34). Herbert came to be connected with the court, and he seemed destined for a worldly career; however he entered holy orders and, under Archbishop Laud's influence, ministered at Bemerton in Wiltshire. Like his friend Nicholas Ferrar (see page 47) he represents, in his life and works, the counter-challenge of the Laudian party to the Puritans.

Scientists too were flourishing, such as William Gilbert (St John's; see page 57), William Harvey (Gilbert & Caius; see page 83) and before long, Isaac Newton (Trinity College; see page 81).

royal visits, cost dear. At his death in 1604, Sir Henry left the house and lands to his older son, Sir Oliver, the largest farm being left to the second son, Robert, father of Oliver Cromwell. Sir Oliver (the Protector's uncle) continued to entertain in style until financial reasons forced him to sell the estate in 1627. It was bought by the 1st Earl of Sandwich (a Montagu), whose personal assistant for a time was Samuel Pepys. Born at Brampton nearby,

Pepys later went to Magdalene College, Cambridge (see page 19).

Oliver himself was born in 1599 and entered Sidney Sussex College in April 1616. A year later Oliver's father died and he was recalled to run the family farm. In 1628 he became MP for Huntingdon and in 1640 for Cambridge; later he lived in Ely in what is now the Tourist Office. Once the Eastern Association had been set up to tighten Parliament's control, East Anglia became the Parliamentarian heartland where Cromwell raised his New Model Army, made up of sturdy but God-fearing men who, in his words, 'as had the fear of God before them and as made some conscience of what they did… the plain russet-coated captain that knows what he fights for and loves what he knows [ie the word of God].'

During the Civil War, which commenced in 1642 when the king raised his standard at Nottingham, the Cambridge colleges largely supported the Royalists, whereas the town was pro-Parliament. The Parliamentarian army reinforced their stronghold at Cambridge castle with stone taken from other sites including the demolished bridge of Clare College. Parliamentarian forces attacking Royalists inside St John's College destroyed the gates of the main entrance tower, and those now in place are the gates installed in 1662. Captain Docwra of Fulbourn marched in with his troop to intercept the King's College plate which Charles I had called for to swell the Royalist money chests.

In 1643, the 2nd Earl of Manchester dispatched General Dowsing to East Anglia for the purpose of rooting out all 'medieval superstition' from churches and chapels. Every college chapel was visited. Statues and stained glass images of saints were broken or removed. No college chapel was left untouched save the Puritan colleges of Emmanuel (1584) and Sidney Sussex (1596), and also Corpus Christi (1352), founded on behalf of Cambridge citizens by two town guilds (see page 35).

Oliver Cromwell died in 1658, but Charles II ordered his soldiers to dig up his coffin in Westminster Abbey, sever the head from the body and, as a warning to others, display the head on the top of a pike outside the entrance of Parliament. It remained here for nineteen years before being sold and resold for increasingly high prices until it was bought by the Wilkinson family in 1818 who gave it to Sidney Sussex in 1960.

One of Cromwell's great supporters was the poet John Milton (Christ's College, and the writer of 'Paradise Lost' and 'Paradise Regained'). He wrote pamphlets on behalf of the Parliamentarian cause, and his Areopagitica is a clear call for freedom of worship, freedom of conscience and freedom of the press—another claim for democracy, which the

Left: The Pepys Library, Magdalene College

Reformation had been so instrumental in launching.

During the period of the Commonwealth and Protectorate it became obligatory to use the Presbyterian Directory instead of the Prayer Book. On one occasion, Cromwell is alleged to have entered Great St Mary's during a service to find the Prayer Book in use. This he destroyed on the chancel steps in view of those assembled.

King's Chapel

Apart from Emmanuel, Sidney Sussex and Corpus Christi, King's chapel was the only college to come out of the Civil War comparatively unscathed, although Parliamentarian troops did use it for a while as a drill hall and even profaned it to the extent that they temporarily stabled horses there. Cromwell would hardly have endorsed that, but some local commanders had fewer scruples. Inside, near the east end of the north wall, graffiti left by Parliamentarian soldiers depicts a mounted Ironside cantering his steed; it remains visible though blurred with the passage of time. Charred chicken bones, dice and cards have also been recovered from beneath the stalls, the latter possibly resulting from bored students attending lengthy chapel services. However, General Dowsing did visit the chapel on Christmas Eve, 1643, though mercifully nothing happened. There are conflicting views as to why it went untouched: perhaps the destruction of the enormous windows would effectively destroy a Christian

Above: Oliver Cromwell in a window of Emmanuel United Reformed Church

Below: The extensive gardens of Emmanuel College with the pond, encircled by shrubs, in which the Dominicans fished for their supper

place of worship, which was never the Parliamentarians' intention; alternatively, since it was Christmas Eve, Dowsing may have had his own family festivities to consider and left the task to someone else who never completed the work.

Henry VI, who founded King's in the 15th century and personally determined the chapel's design, sought to glorify God, not himself. A pious man better suited to monastic life, Henry lost the crowns of France and England, before being thrown into the Tower of London in 1461 and murdered there ten years later.

The four kings who succeeded him were more addicted to their own glory than to God's, though keen to appear to endorse Henry VI's godly work. They thus continued to contribute to the chapel's construction, whilst using it to publicise themselves. King's chapel is the finest example of Gothic Perpendicular architecture (though the stained glass is Renaissance), and has both the largest fan-vault as well as the finest complete collection of original Renaissance stained glass in the world. The glass was the work of Flemish artists, the wood carving that of French and Italians. The building itself took 101 years to complete.

Modern architects are amazed that King's chapel still stands, given that its foundations descend a mere metre and a half. As at Hampton Court, broken oyster

Top: The interior of Emmanuel College chapel which, apart from its stained glass, is as it was on completion in 1674. Amigoni's 'Return of the Prodigal Son' hangs behind the altar

Above: Sidney Sussex College chapel with the Franciscan shield (right). The wooden Cross is green, since wood is green when alive. Thus it's through the Cross that we attain eternal life

Left: King's chapel from the River Cam and the 'Backs'

shell, mixed in the mortar below ground level, provides an effective damp-proof course, whilst the building itself has survived huge winds and storms being perfectly balanced along its entire length. Limestone varies in its density dependent on its geographic source, thus two stones with the same dimensions can vary in weight. The masons therefore cut each stone in two precisely and inserted both halves immediately opposite each other in the two great facades.

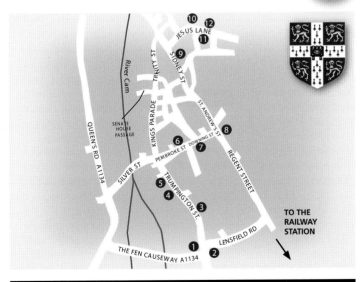

CAMBRIDGE: MUSEUMS AND FURTHER PURITAN ESTABLISHMENTS

KEY

1 ROYAL CAMBRIDGE HOTEL
2 HOBSON'S CONDUIT (FOUNTAIN)
3 'OLD ADDENBROOKES' HOSPITAL
4 THE FITZWILLIAM MUSEUM
5 LITTLE ST. MARY'S CHURCH
6 ZOOLOGY MUSEUM
7 GEOLOGY MUSEUM
8 EMMANUEL COLLEGE
9 SIDNEY SUSSEX COLLEGE
10 WESLEY HOUSE (THEOLOGICAL) COLL.
11 WESTCOTT HOUSE (THEOLOGICAL) COLL.
12 JESUS COLLEGE

Begin outside the Royal Cambridge Hotel opposite Hobson's conduit and fountain, and turn left up Trumpington Street tracing the course of the conduit's two extensions. You will pass on your right Old Addenbrooke's Hospital, now the University Department of Management Studies.

On your left looms the highly impressive facade of the:

Fitzwilliam Museum

www.fitzmuseum.cam.ac.uk
✆ 01223 332900

One of the best museums in the country outside London, and recently extended. It has paintings by the Impressionists, German armour, Japanese prints, Egyptology and much else. Entrance is free; it has excellent facilities including a new cafeteria.

Next you pass Peterhouse on the left, the first college to be founded (1284). Beyond it you reach:

Top left: Little St Mary's Church, which previously lay outside the city boundary

Bottom left: Godfrey Washington's memorial in Little St Mary's with the stars and stripes of the Washington family arms

Little St Mary's Church

Trumpington Street, Cambridge, CB2 1QG
www.lsm.org.uk
✆ 01223 366202

The church is open by day and has a natural wild garden in its graveyard. There has been a church on this site since at least the 12th century; parts of it remain in the current church, which dates from 1352. Originally named 'St Peter's without Trumpington Gate', it stood outside the medieval town's southern gate and the 'King's Ditch'; this ditch, though no longer apparent, ringed the town on the south and east, the River Cam guarding the other two approaches. Inside Little St Mary's is the tomb of Godfrey Washington (d. 1729), George Washington's great-uncle. The Washington family arms (displayed inside the church) later became the 'Stars and Stripes' of the U.S.A. Godfrey was the minister of the church and bursar of Peterhouse, to which college the church was physically linked when the church once served as a 'collegiate parish church', before the college built its own.

Continue past Emmanuel United Reformed Church (left) and Pembroke College (right) and turn right up Pembroke Street/Downing Street. Continue walking past the University Museums of Zoology (left) and Geology (right), which both exhibit material Charles Darwin sent back during his voyage round the world.

Emmanuel College

St Andrew's Street, Cambridge, CB2 3AP
www.emma.cam.ac.uk
✆ 01223 334200

Many Puritans, including emigrants to New England, came to a 'reformed' faith while here. The chapter above lists some of the best known. Be sure to step inside the chapel designed by Sir Christopher Wren and view the great men who feature in the stained glass, inserted in the 1880s.

Proceed north, first via Christ's College (if not already visited, see page 33 Travel Information for main details). John Milton's and Charles Darwin's rooms for part of their time at Cambridge were both in First Court. Continue up Sidney Street to Sidney Sussex College.

Sidney Sussex College

Sidney Street, Cambridge, CB2 3HU
www.sid.cam.ac.uk
✆ 01223 338800

This was previously the Franciscan site, the college being founded in 1596. The gardens, reached through Cloister Court, are beautiful. The ante-chapel has stained glass originating from the Franciscans and a plaque which tells the reader that Oliver Cromwell's head is buried nearby (see page 74). The inscription (three words run together) over the Pittoni painting of 'The Holy Family' behind the altar bears the wording 'Gustando vivimus Deo', meaning 'We live by tasting God', a direct reference to the sacrament of the Eucharist.

Turn right out of the college and right again up Jesus Lane, passing the theological colleges Westcott House (Anglican) and Wesley College (Methodist) till you reach Jesus College.

Jesus College

Jesus Lane, Cambridge, CB5 8BL
www.jesus.cam.ac.uk
✆ 01223 339339

Originally a Benedictine nunnery 1136–1496, it became the alma mater of Thomas Cranmer, John Eliot (who translated the Algonquin Bible), Samuel Taylor Coleridge, T.R. Malthus (pioneer of the science of political economy) and the current Prince Edward. Jesus College is alone among colleges in having its sports grounds alongside its buildings.

Above: The plaque in Sidney Sussex antechapel commemorating the reburial of Oliver Cromwell's head

❻ Modern Science and the Age of Reason

The seeds of the Thirty Years War in Europe and of the Civil War in England were sown in the 16th century Reformation and Counter Reformation. By 1650 Europe was exhausted and people now shunned debate on divine revelation in favour of discussion inspired by the power of human 'reason' and the rise in empirical science and philosophy

The 'Modern' scientists of the 17th century were almost all religious men. They did their science within their theological understanding of God's world. God, they thought, had been totally rational in his Creation and had applied the laws of nature logically, so that the two disciplines dovetailed. Furthermore, God had implanted in the human race the faculty of reason so that we ourselves can be logical. If therefore, a scientist knew 'a', and could discover 'b', he would automatically arrive at 'c' in a step-by-step progression. These scientists believed God wanted man to discover the habitat in which he was placed, and for these 17th century scientists, doing science became an act of worship. Isaac Newton once wrote, 'God is the God of order, and not of confusion', which echoes Kepler's words as he sought to establish the orbit of the planet Mars; Kepler got it wrong but he knew that he not only could but would rectify his error if he applied himself to the task. As he sought the answer

and realised that he was nearing the correct solution—which took him eight years—he cried out: 'O God, I am thinking thy thoughts after thee.' This belief in divine Creation is to be found again in Newton's magnum opus *Principia Mathematica* (1687), which was edited and financed by Edmond Halley of comet fame; Newton declared: 'I shall make no discovery, unless it is imparted to me by the Holy Spirit'.

However, by the mid 17th century the philosophical mood of the western world was changing, and society as a whole had grown tired of debating religious doctrine. Trust in revelation diminished, whilst increasingly the supernatural was denied. People now began to focus on the power of human 'reason'.

Facing page: The apple tree, standing outside Trinity College, a genuine descendant of the tree at Woolsthorpe, Lincs, under which Isaac Newton sat

Philosophy and science

Through the 17th and 18th centuries, first rational philosophy (the use of reason) and then empirical philosophy (the use of observation) was enthusiastically pursued. So too was 'Modern Science', a phrase referring to a change in scientific method: instead of the 'deductive' method of advancing hypotheses and trying to establish facts to fit the hypotheses, scientists reversed the process by following an 'inductive' method, which meant starting from a basis of observation, and only then establishing the theory ('empirical science'). This was the scientific method of Galileo, who embraced Copernican theory (the earth goes round the sun, not vice versa, as previously believed). Galileo was branded a heretic by the church and, facing torture, he recanted. Johannes Kepler (the German astronomer who established the laws of planetary motion) was also an empirical scientist, and so, a little later (born in 1642) was Isaac Newton (Trinity College).

Cambridge experienced this shift of focus and change in philosophical mood. Francis Bacon (Trinity College, a contemporary of Galileo and Kepler, and later in life Lord Chancellor of England under James I), was a major philosopher of the early 17th century and was extremely influential in urging scientists to pursue empirical science in order to obtain factual evidence that could be used to produce realistic theories. His influence was felt in Cambridge and England in his life-time, not least by Isaac Newton, and on the European continent for a century after his death. It must not be forgotten, however, that Bacon was a believer in God, just as Galileo, Kepler and Newton were. Indeed he believed that no man could be too well versed in the two books of God: the book of God's word (the Bible) and, metaphorically, the book of God's works (Nature). He stressed the latter to such extent that he inadvertently failed to do justice to the former, thus helping to influence men towards science rather than religion. Unfortunately Bacon's thoughts on experimentation led him to stuff a goose with snow in an attempt to preserve it. He waited before eating it—and promptly died!

Left: Francis Bacon's statue in Trinity College chapel, a genius but a flawed character, whose corruptibility is brilliantly evoked in this statue

Two great experimental scientists

William Harvey, who studied at Gonville and Caius (see page 63) becoming Royal Physician to Charles II and Warden of Merton College Oxford, was a great experimental physician, publishing his treatise in 1628 which explained how blood circulates in the body. He is also known as the 'Father of Embryology'. John Ray, another empirical scientist (a student and Fellow of Trinity College), was also a great Christian, ready to defend his convictions. He lost his post as a Fellow in 1662 when he refused to take the oath of the Anglican Church's Act of Uniformity after the Restoration. He originated the basic forms of plant classification into cryptogams, monocotyledons and diocotyledons. His zoological work, in which he developed the most natural pre-Linnaean classification of the animal kingdom, has been considered of even greater importance than his botanical achievements. The Christian conservation organisation today, the John Ray Initiative, is named after him.

Above: William Harvey, holding a human heart, opposite Gonville and Caius, his old college

Below: Trinity College bridge, rebuilt in stone in 1765 by James Essex

Overleaf: Isaac Newton's birthplace at Woolsthorpe Manor, Lincs, now houses the Isaac Newton Heritage Museum

Isaac Newton's early life

Isaac Newton was born in 1642 at Woolsthorpe. His father died before he was born, and his mother remarried and moved elsewhere when he was only three. Isaac, who was then brought up by his grandmother and aunt, had no siblings and was a lonely child; he had permanent difficulty, even as an adult, in engaging with other people. Sent to school in Grantham, where he lodged with an apothecary above his shop in the High Street and whose potions Newton viewed with interest, he arrived at Trinity College in 1662 at the age of nineteen. This contrasted with the average age of most new students, who were considerably younger and had never been to school; they had to be brought up to a minimum educational level before embarking on a degree course, which in turn meant they remained many years at the University. Newton however started to study for his degree from the outset.

Newton entered Trinity as a 'sizar', the lowest class of student who had to offset his fees in part by doing menial tasks around the college, including serving the 'Fellow Commoners' (sons of the nobility) at table. Isaac was converted to Christianity in his first year by Isaac Barrow (Master of Trinity College, 1672–1677), and went on to obtain his degree in 1665, the year that the Great Plague, chronicled by Samuel Pepys, spread from London to Cambridge. Cambridge, situated on the banks of a highly polluted river—effectively an open sewer—posed health hazards to academics and townspeople alike. Whenever the plague returned, the University closed until the danger was past. Students returned home or stayed with friends. The college Fellows, who were obliged to remain celibate, had no homes (their colleges being home to them), and thus they moved temporarily into farms and manors bequeathed to their colleges. Newton went home to Woolsthorpe and remained there for some twenty-one months.

During this interim period he produced some of his best work. Interested in optics, he used the prism he had bought at Stourbridge Fair (see page 10) to refract the light passing through

the window of his room and to produce the spectrum of colours we see in a rainbow. He also worked out the universal law of gravity. The story of the apple tree is totally authentic: the tree in question fell in a gale in 1820, but left a stump well rooted in the ground from which there grew the tree now seen at Woolsthorpe; the tree outside Trinity College is one of several cuttings taken in 1956, and has been DNA tested!

Newton was a difficult man. Held in awe but with few friends, he was often involved in controversy. Later he was party to a heated exchange of views with Leibniz as to which of them had first invented differential calculus and the 'method of fluxions'. The Oxford scientist Robert Hooke claimed priority of discovery for some of Newton's work on the attraction of lunar bodies. John Flamsteed (Jesus College), the first Astronomer Royal at Greenwich, was another to be embroiled in disputes with Newton, although Flamsteed's *Greenwich Observations*, published by Newton, provided some of the data Newton needed for his work.

Newton's alchemy and other science

When Newton returned to Cambridge in 1667 as a Fellow of Trinity College, he lived at the front of the college overlooking a garden given to him by the college in which he grew the flowers he needed for his experiments. In 1668 he was appointed Lucasian Professor of Mathematics, a chair later held by Stephen Hawking, the famous cosmologist. It was also in 1668 that Newton started working in alchemy, a practice to which he makes scant reference since alchemy was outlawed at that time; how, after all, could anyone translate base metal into gold from the crucible, or obtain from it the 'elixir of life', an essence that supposedly ensured perpetual youth? Such things smacked of black magic and witchcraft and were therefore outlawed. Newton took the risk because he believed God had given him grace to discover the basic law of Creation in the crucible, and then to make it known to the world, after which he would solve all the other laws of nature through mathematics. He worked for 25 years in this pursuit in a wooden laboratory in the corner of his garden against the college chapel's north wall, but success eluded him and he fell ill in 1693 through overwork. By then he had written *Principia Mathematica*, the first version

Right: 'Principia Mathematica'; the first version is displayed in the Wren Library at Trinity College

of which is kept in the magnificent Christopher Wren designed Library at the back of Trinity College; the pencilled margin notes are those Newton wrote as he prepared it for the second edition. In addition he constructed a reflecting telescope of the type later developed by the astronomer William Herschel, whose son, also an astronomer, was a student and Fellow of St John's College.

Above: The Master's Lodge, Trinity College, where Queen Anne knighted Sir Isaac Newton

Below: The Wren Library front facade seen from across Nevile's Court

In 1696 Newton left for London, where he became Master of the Royal Mint. During his tenure of the post some twenty-eight counterfeiters were hanged—this was regarded by society as more than satisfactory proof of Newton's ability as an administrator! He rarely returned to Woolsthorpe or to Cambridge, except when he became MP for Cambridge University in 1701. Two years later he was appointed President of the Royal Society. The Society had received its charter in 1662 for the advancement of science and the first secretary was John Wilkins, Master of Trinity College, though he was dispossessed of his Mastership at the Restoration of the monarchy because of his Puritan views.

In 1705 Queen Anne knighted Newton in the Master's Lodge of Trinity College. Newton's best scientific days were now behind him, and in the last thirty years of his life, his interest swung

Right: The interior of the Wren Library looking towards Thorvaldsen's statue of Lord Byron, rejected earlier by Westminster Abbey on the grounds of his disreputable life-style

increasingly away from science and towards religion. He wrote commentaries on the biblical books of Daniel and Revelation, and even built a model of King Solomon's Temple as recorded in the Bible. Isaac Newton died in 1727 at the age of eighty-five and was buried in Westminster Abbey. A visitor will find Alexander Pope's epithet at Newton's home (Woolsthorpe Manor, Lincs), the two-line verse being a play on the first chapter of Genesis 'Nature and Nature's laws were hid in night; God said "Let Newton be", and all was light'.

In Cambridge meanwhile, John Dryden had started his poetical career at Trinity College. He is considered transitional between the metaphysical poets (see page 73) and the neo-classic reaction which he did so much to create.

Trinity also produced Judge Jeffreys (1648–1689). Called to the Bar in 1668, he rose rapidly, was knighted in 1677 and became Chief Justice of the King's Bench six years later. Among his earliest trials, he presided at those of Titus Oates and the Puritan Richard Baxter. In every State trial he proved a willing tool of the crown. He was eventually raised to the peerage by James II in 1685, following his service to the king earlier that year by stamping out the 'Monmouth Rebellion' in the south-west led by the Duke of Monmouth. The latter, an illegitimate son of Charles II, had branded James II a popish usurper and attempted to seize the crown. The severity of the sentences on the rebels handed out by Jeffreys, earned him the name of 'Hanging' Jeffreys, while his courts became known as the 'Bloody Assizes'.

The Restoration of the Monarchy

In 1688 the avowedly Catholic King James II was forced to abdicate, an event referred to as 'The Glorious Revolution' since no blood was shed. England's fledgling democratic institutions were viewed enthusiastically by the French outcast Voltaire who championed Protestantism and religious toleration. England, already launched on the early stages of a constitutional monarchy, proceeded to the modern style of parliament under Robert Walpole who became Chancellor of the Exchequer in 1715 and as such is considered to be the first Prime Minister of

Above: *Thomas Gray's window at Peterhouse, with his improvised fire escape*

Great Britain. The Act of Union had united Scotland with England and Wales in 1707. King George I (1714–1727) was a Hanoverian who could speak no English and this meant that Walpole was left at considerable liberty to chair a small group of ministers, the forerunner of today's Cabinet. Earlier, Walpole had been a student at King's College, as was his son Horace who, following his 'Grand Tour' of Europe which lasted two and a half years and on which he was accompanied by the poet Thomas Gray, later became a writer, MP and art collector.

Thomas Gray, who wrote 'Elegy on a Country Churchyard' ('The curfew tolls the knell of parting day, the lowing herd winds slowly o'er the lea …'), was a student at Peterhouse. Gray had a horror of fires and his room in Peterhouse was on the top floor;

there being no emergency fire exit nearby, he had an iron frame built outside his window to which he attached one end of a long rope. In the event of fire, he therefore had a ready means of escape. This became known, and one night fellow students, who often ragged him, started to yell 'Fire! Fire!' from within the building. Up went the window and down came Thomas, landing not on the grass below but in a tub of cold water placed to greet his arrival. So upset was he, that he immediately applied for a transfer to Pembroke College, which was granted.

Declining standards

Despite the Evangelical Revival in Britain, which paralleled the 'Great Awakening' in North America, people in general now chose to place their faith, not on religion, but on science and the power of human 'reason' in order to achieve knowledge and understanding. The 18th century is therefore known as the 'Age of Enlightenment' or the 'Age of Reason', and it witnessed a serious decline in true religion. Eventually the folly of this approach led to the French Revolution, and the 19th century Modernist Society (see page 121).

This century also saw a sharp decline in academic standards at the universities of Oxford, Cambridge and Trinity College, Dublin, though less so in Scottish universities. As the British Empire stretched across the oceans, so young men, the sons of gentry, set up commercial enterprises to profit from the trading available. The Industrial Revolution—

which began in the 1770s and tripled the nation's wealth within a generation—lessened the need for a university education. To start a company or to build a factory required no degree or paper qualification, and this had the effect of devaluing all degrees. An attitude arose that if degrees did not matter, why bother? The sons of the leisured classes who did attend university had the right to receive degrees on completion of the course without examination. Not so the poorer students. Young men, however, like Byron (see page 95) and Wilberforce (see page 95), who at that stage was neither interested in abolishing slavery nor being a Christian, spent their waking hours playing cards, dicing and drinking. Looking back years later Wilberforce described his time at Cambridge as 'shapeless idleness', and this was not untypical of his day. Some students went hunting and the memorial to a stag pursued and killed inside St John's College First Court is testimony to a leisured era. 'Chair' holders like William Lax, Professor of Astronomy and Geometry for

Top right: The Gibbs Fellows Building (1732) in King's College. Charles Simeon used to pray on the roof-top 'unseen by all but God', starting as early as four o'clock in the morning

Right: The Senate House, the centre of the University, built by James Gibbs in 1730

forty-two years, drew the stipend for lectures which they never once gave. This lamentable scenario continued until the mid 19th century (see page 100).

Charles Simeon at Cambridge

The Evangelical Revival of the 18th century had little impact on Cambridge. George Whitfield and John and Charles Wesley were Oxford men, and the nearest John Wesley came to Cambridge was Harston, to its immediate south, when on his way to Walsingham in Norfolk, the site of a famous shrine for medieval pilgrims. Cambridge religiosity slumped despite the work of William Paley of Christ's College, who was not an original thinker but a sublime expositor of the theology of others.

In 1779, however, Charles Simeon arrived at King's College. He was born in 1759, the same year as William Wilberforce and William Pitt (the Younger); Pitt had arrived at Pembroke College, aged 14, and ten years later became Britain's youngest Prime Minister guiding his country through the French Revolution and the early part of the Napoleonic threat. It was Pitt who introduced Income Tax in support of the war effort, promising to remove it after the war. He died before the end of the war and the fulfilment of his promise.

Simeon's influence, meanwhile, would ultimately change the Cambridge theology syllabus, raise the competence of men entering the church and inspire many missionaries (see page 97). Even after his death, his influence was shown in the response to David Livingstone's call for young men to join him in Africa, and also in the setting up of two Cambridge theological seminaries later in the 19th century. It is possible also to ascribe to his legacy the decision by seven young men (known as the 'Cambridge Seven', see page 97) to leave England in the early 1880s for distant China and the formation of the China Inland Mission, following the work there of Hudson Taylor.

Simeon's early incumbency at Holy Trinity Church, Cambridge, was hardly propitious to a fruitful ministry. His church wardens locked him out of his own church because they and most of the congregation had wanted the previous curate to fill the post. Simeon often sought consolation on the shoulder of Henry Venn (father of John Venn, chaplain to the Clapham Sect, see page 95). His problem was that he was young, and rather apt to tell others where they fell short. He also had too much religion to meet the approval of an increasingly secular society. The townspeople then joined in. As

Above: Downing College's neo-classical architecture

Simeon's growing influence

On Friday evenings, Simeon would invite any Cambridge student to meet in his rooms in King's for discussions of a biblical, moral or spiritual nature. He showed them how to preach expository sermons on biblical texts, and sent them to the county gaol on Castle Hill to talk to prisoners and so gain pastoral experience. Simeon set up the Jesus Lane Sunday School in the late 1820s for students to teach the local tykes (ragamuffins) about Jesus and Christian morality. He was a co-founder of the Church Missionary Society and of the Church Mission to the Jews; and he also laid the ground for the eventual birth of the CICCU (The Cambridge Inter-Collegiate Christian Union) which led to the establishment of similar organisations world-wide (see page 120).

His family being well off, Simeon bought up 'church livings' (which gave him the right to nominate new incumbents) placing in them some of those students he had instructed; by his death in 1836 the Simeon Trust controlled around forty livings—today it controls over 150. By his death Simeon had given away most of his money, often to villagers around Cambridge who suffered from poor harvests.

The historian T.B. Macaulay wrote that Simeon could easily have asked for a transfer or become a bishop. His influence on the religion of this country, was, Macaulay continued, greater than that of anyone after John Wesley. In the margins of his Bible against 1 Corinthians I:27–29, 'God hath chosen the foolish things of this world to confound the wise …' Simeon wrote, 'If there is a man who understands and who is ready (to be such an instrument of Christ), it is I. I am the man to set my seal to that text, I am ready, I am he'. Various of his papers and his collection of sermons which inspired so many students in his day and since are held jointly in the libraries of King's College and Ridley Hall Theological College where they continue to inspire those preparing for ordination. Simeon's remains are stored in the very shallow crypt in King's College.

he passed between Holy Trinity and King's, stall holders in the market pelted him with rotten produce. Yet he bore it, believing it to be the particular work and the right place to which Christ had called him. His congregation largely dispersed and went to other churches. Some ten years later, most of his flock returned, realising the true goodness in the man. He remained in the same post to the day he died—in all fifty-four years.

In spite of the efforts of Simeon, the century closed with the founding of Downing College (1800), the first college foundation for over 200 years and thoroughly representative of its time. Its endowment was squandered in litigation, typifying much of society's grabbing mentality, it was financed on the back of the slave trade, and its architecture was classical, a throw-back to the pagan Greeks and Romans.

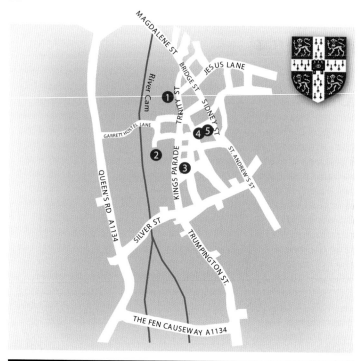

CAMBRIDGE: IN THE FOOTSTEPS OF BACON, NEWTON AND SIMEON

KEY

1 TRINITY COLLEGE
2 KING'S COLLEGE
  CHAPEL ENTRANCE

3 THE COPPER KETTLE
4 DON PASQUALE
  RESTAURANT

5 HOLY TRINITY CHURCH

TRAVEL INFORMATION

Trinity College

Trinity Street, Cambridge,
CB2 1TQ
www.trin.cam.ac.uk
✆ 01223 338400

This was Henry VIII's foundation in 1546. It is the largest college with over 1000 students, and by far the wealthiest of all Oxford and Cambridge colleges. It has produced countless famous men in all spheres of life.

Francis Bacon and Isaac Newton were here. Trinity has fashioned prime ministers, archbishops, scientists, judges, poets and composers; the list and variety is endless, not to mention 31 Nobel Prize winners. Try to visit the Wren Library and the Dining Hall, which is modelled on Middle Temple's refectory in London. It is still a Royal College and any appointment to the Mastership needs the monarch's approval.

Edward VII, George VI and Prince Charles all studied here. Discover the array of statues and plaques in the antechapel and the portraits in the Dining Hall. The Wren Library holds Newton's first version of *Principia Mathematica*, Milton's poems and A.A. Milne's manuscript version of *Winnie the Pooh*. Milne and his son Christopher Robin were both alumni here.

Left: *Simeon's rooms lay behind the huge Diocletian window over the Jumbo arch of the Gibb's Building, King's College*

King's College

King's Parade, Cambridge, CB2 1ST
www.kings.cam.ac.uk
☏ 01223 331100

Its superb Gothic Perpendicular chapel (see page 6) is open throughout the year, except when rehearsals or recordings are being held. It closes at marginally variable hours in the afternoon, but Evensong during term time is open to the public. Alumni include Robert Walpole, Maynard Keynes (the economist), Charles Simeon (see above), the novelist E.M. Forster and Rupert Brooke the poet.

The Copper Kettle, 4 King's Parade, offers a good cup of coffee or hot food before you set off across the Market Square to Holy Trinity Church. Alternatively there is the restaurant 'Don Pasquale' on the corner where Market Street opens out onto Market Square.

predecessor was burnt down by one of the many fires starting in the Market Square. This was Charles Simeon's church; its plaques commemorate many of the missionaries he inspired, including Henry Martyn (see page 97).

Holy Trinity Church

Market Street, Cambridge, CB2 3NZ
www.htcambridge.org.uk
☏ 01223 355397

Intercom entry from Market Street. The present church has stood here since 1174, when its

Middle: *Charles Simeon in the pulpit of Holy Trinity Church*

Bottom: *Holy Trinity Church in the 18th century; here Simeon served faithfully throughout his entire working life*

7 Missionaries, social reformers and scientists

The Enlightenment, driven by science and the power of human 'reason' produced the 19th century 'mechanistic' society. Despite the Romantic backlash, and the work of social reformers in Britain and missionaries abroad, the victory of science and 'reason' seemed assured

Increasingly in the 19th century, particularly after Darwinian theory made its impact in the century's third quarter, people came to believe that man would not only know everything there was to know about the world, but also be in a position to control it. The demise of this outlook would occur later, but first it provoked a strong reaction among the Romantic writers, who looked beyond the purely 'mechanistic' interpretation of life and sought to express their emotions in nature and childhood, realising that there was another dimension to life even if it wasn't a religious one. Cambridge produced William Wordsworth (St John's), Samuel Taylor Coleridge (Jesus College), and both Byron and later Tennyson (at Trinity College).

Wilberforce and social reform
The social reform of the 19th century was the fruit of a general evangelical revival in the 18th, and was characterised by a range of initiatives on the part of reformers to improve conditions for the socially disadvantaged. The main impetus for this reform came from William Wilberforce (St John's 1776–1779) and those assisting him in the drive to abolish slavery. Wilberforce has been called 'the greatest social reformer in history.' He was the key member of the 'Clapham Sect', based in South London, which looked to improve standards in many areas including education and prison reform, though their main target was the abolition of the slave trade across the Atlantic, following which the spotlight fell on slavery itself. When Parliament finally passed an Act abolishing slavery in July 1833, Wilberforce lay dying but conscious; he died a happy man, having learnt that his forty-four year parliamentary campaign, had succeeded. There were distinct secondary effects. France and Spain both abolished slavery in the 1840s; the United States did so in 1865 at the end of their Civil War.

Opposite page: The historian T.B. Macaulay's statue in Trinity College ante-chapel

Slavery, however, was far from his only achievement. Wilberforce and those who worked with him had been engaged in raising the moral conscience of the people of Britain, something they termed 'The Reformation of Manners'. (See in this series *William Wilberforce—the friend of humanity* by Kevin Belmonte). As a result, in the first half of the 19th century, Factory Acts were passed limiting the hours women and children could be forced to work in factories, whilst the 1832 Reform Bill aimed at a fairer parliamentary representation of the British people. Education of children received attention, as did subsequent improvements in housing, and also refuse and sewage disposal; British health benefited to the extent that its population of 10 million in 1800 quadrupled in a century.

Two men in particular who supported Wilberforce in the cause of Abolition were Thomas Clarkson and the African Olaudah Equiano; Equiano was a slave who later

Left: Thomas Clarkson's statue on the outside of St John's College chapel: being a liberator, he holds a loosened chain, whilst its key lies at his feet

Below: The plaque at St Andrew's Church (Chesterton) commemorating Anna Maria, the daughter of Olaudah Equiano, alias Gustavus Vassa. The epitaph was composed by Martha Peckard, wife of the Master of Magdalene College

Near this Place lies Interred
ANNA MARIA VASSA.
Daughter of GUSTAVUS VASSA the AFRICAN.
She died July 21. 1797.
Aged 4 Years.

Should simple village rhymes attract thine eye,
Stranger, as thoughtfully thou passest by,
Know that there lies beside this humble stone
A child of colour haply not thine own.
Her father born of Afric's sun-burnt race,
Torn from his native fields, ah foul disgrace:

gained his freedom and wrote *The Interesting Narrative of the Life of Olaudah Equiano, or Gustavus Vassa, the African* (1789). This related his first-hand experiences on board a slave ship and life as a slave; it was hugely popular, and ran to twelve editions. As for Clarkson, a local man from Wisbech, north of Cambridge, who became a student at St John's just as Wilberforce was leaving, it is true to say that if Clarkson could never have achieved what Wilberforce accomplished, neither could the latter have succeeded without Clarkson's enormous input. In seven years Clarkson rode 35,000 miles round Britain, addressing gatherings, raising anti-slavery societies and urging boroughs to petition Parliament to end slavery. He visited the docks at London, Bristol and Liverpool and interviewed 20,000 sailors about their experiences on slave ships. It was he who provided the statistics which Wilberforce used as ammunition in his speeches. Only in recent years has Clarkson been commemorated with a plaque in Westminster Abbey.

But what sparked the whole movement? Earlier in the 18th century the Quakers had agitated for abolition. Being Nonconformists and debarred from seats in Parliament, they had no political platform from which to make themselves heard. The all-important factor in directing Wilberforce's attention onto slavery was the Latin essay on its evil which Clarkson wrote in 1785 as part of an essay competition in Cambridge. It won the competition and Wilberforce saw a published version of it the following year—the fuse was lit.

Charles Simeon's influence on missionary work

One of Wilberforce's Cambridge contemporaries had been Charles Simeon (King's College) who, as we saw in the previous chapter, left such an imprint on the religious life of Cambridge and whose influence was felt far and wide. Many missionaries leaving this country during and after his life time came under that influence. Emerging from the evangelical hot-house of Magdalene College, where Peter Peckard, its Master, exerted his own considerable influence as well, were David Brown (to India), Richard Johnson (Australia), and Samuel Marsden ('the Apostle of New Zealand'). Daniel Corrie (Clare College) and Claudius Buchanan (Queens' College) both went to India under Simeon's influence. Shortly afterwards Henry Martyn (St John's College) became chaplain to the East India Company, translating the Bible into Hindustani; he was replaced at his death by Thomas Thomason (Magdalene College). John Barton (Christ's College) left for India later in the 19th century. One of the consequences of Simeon's on-going influence was the departure of the 'Cambridge Seven' for China where they were to work with the China Inland Mission. Society in Britain failed to understand how young men could turn their backs on bright futures at home in order to go so far afield to help people to whom the nation felt no obligation. It even seemed unpatriotic. One of the Seven was the Test cricketer, C.T. Studd (Trinity College), who had participated in the 1882 series against Australia in which England lost the 'Ashes' for the first time.

Christian Socialists

Charles Kingsley (Magdalene College), known for his poetry and other writing, was later appointed Professor of Modern History at Cambridge; he was an example of 'muscular Christianity'; together with F.D. Maurice (Trinity College) he became a leader in the Christian Socialist movement attempting to raise the lot of the working classes. Though Maurice had followed the university curriculum, he had been ineligible for a degree because he was a non-conformist; since 1613 acceptance of the Thirty-nine Articles was a precondition for government posts and graduating with a degree, and thus Roman Catholics and nonconformists had been excluded. (see page 55). This changed in 1829 when the Catholic Emancipation Act was passed allowing Catholics back into parliament and government posts. However, they and the nonconformists were still unable to gain degrees at Cambridge until 1895, although the Test Act (1871) had officially cleared the way. In 1895 the 1st Baron Acton, a liberal Roman Catholic, was appointed Professor of Modern History at Cambridge, his father having studied previously at Magdalene College, though without taking a degree since he was a Catholic; later he became a Cardinal. As for F.D. Maurice, he later took holy orders in the Church of England and, after working in London, returned to Cambridge as an Honorary Fellow of Trinity Hall, becoming its chaplain. His name features on the list of incumbents in St Edward's Church where the English Reformation started—a church that is still a 'royal peculiar' (see pages 41, 48).

Above: The plaque in Magdalene College chapel commemorating the missionaries Brown, Johnson and Marsden

Charles Babbage and his contemporaries

William Makepeace Thackeray (Trinity College) left Cambridge without taking a degree but embarked on a successful career writing novels. Charles Babbage (Trinity College and then Peterhouse) devoted much of his life to building two calculating machines, neither of which he completed; the funding necessary for the first was unforthcoming, whilst the second was too ambitious for the mechanical devices of his day. Neither can he really be considered a forerunner of the first digital computer, EDSAC (Electronic Delayed Storage Automatic Calculator), produced by Maurice Wilkes (King's College chapter 8). In truth, the design of EDSAC and subsequent computers owes more

to Alan Turing's early designs (also at King's College), secondly to the design of the Bletchley Park code-breaking machines of World War II also designed by Turing with assistance from others, and to the influence of the ENIAC design being pursued in the United States. Meanwhile, between 1848–1861, Thomas Babington Macaulay (Trinity College), whose father Zachary had been involved in the early attempts to abolish slavery, wrote his 'History of England from the accession of James II'.

Despite considerable advances in social reform in Britain, and regular Sunday attendance at worship, society was becoming increasingly secular as

Above: The sign to the Babbage Lecture theatre on the New Museum site in Cambridge

Left: William Wilberforce's statue in the chapel of St John's College, where he was a student 1776–1779

the century unfolded, especially after Darwinian theory and 'Liberal Theology' took hold. True religion and spirituality were slipping away. Matthew Arnold's 'Dover Beach' makes that very point:

> 'The Sea of Faith
> was once, too, at
> the full; and round
> earth's shore
> lay like the bright
> folds of a girdle
> furl'd.
> But now I only hear
> its melancholy, long,
> withdrawing roar'

Academic system overhauled

In mid century the academic standards which had fallen so low at Cambridge were finally improved. The Royal Commission to Cambridge (1850–1856) ended with the Cambridge Act which took the bulk of the lecturing from the colleges and handed it to the University. At that point, a wholesale construction of lecture halls, laboratories and museums got under way. The museums offered students practical examples of the theory learned in lectures (museums were inaccessible to the public at this time). In addition, a whole new raft of academic subjects became available for study in the closing decades, including Modern Languages, History and Engineering, this being one factor among others which undermined the Divinity Faculty's status in the University (see also page 102).

Further building construction

Many other buildings started to appear. The railways reached Cambridge in 1845, but the station was deliberately sited well

Above: The new Roman Catholic church under construction (1887–1890)

out of town, perhaps because the Vice Chancellor of Cambridge was sure that 'God was not pleased' with the railways. The University Arms Hotel, built mid-way between town and station, profited considerably from the influx of Londoners who came for a week-end. In the late 1880s the huge Catholic Church of 'Our Lady and the English Martyrs' was built alongside Hills Road.

The first two women's colleges opened in 1871 (Newnham) and 1873 (Girton). The politics of the day, however, only heightened female frustration. Ten years later, women students were allowed to attend lectures available to their male counterparts, but they were still not permitted to sit examinations. This had to wait until the 1920s, and the conferment of degrees took longer still.

By the early 19th century the University recognised that if the best was to be coaxed from young adults, they needed physical exercise to compensate the sedentary hours spent on study. In the early years of the University's existence, students had released their pent-up energy with bouts of fisticuffs between 'town and gown'. Later, sports were limited to archery (with butts on Midsummer Common), bowls (all colleges had bowling greens), croquet and an early form of tennis. The more moneyed students could hire horses from stables, whilst colleges had stabling for the Fellows' horses.

That apart, there was the walk to Grantchester and back along the river, a most attractive two mile outing on a summer's day, but scarcely agreeable if repeated regularly in the depths of winter.

From top The Bridge of Sighs linking the 19th century New Court of St John's College with its older buildings

Newnham College gardens and the college buildings, designed in the domestic, neo-Dutch 'Queen Anne' style, which brought an air of femininity to this part of Cambridge

The walk along the river between Newnham and Grantchester

The view across a corner of Midsummer Common to the river and the college boat-houses

Unsurprisingly, it came to be known as the 'Grantchester Grind'. The University Botanic Garden beckoned those wanting a gentle stroll, once moved (1846–1852) by J.S. Henslow (Professor of Botany and Charles Darwin's mentor) from its site off Free School Lane (where it had served as a physic garden) to its present location; even then it only occupied the western half of its current forty acre site.

Secularisation

Behind this burgeoning activity on many fronts, the back-drop was less healthy. Secularisation was fast becoming all-invasive. The Divinity Faculty had not only to contend with the many new disciplines on offer to the students, but was also being undermined by the advent of 'Liberal Theology' which, starting in Germany in the 18th century, had fanned out over Europe. 'Liberal theologians' undermined the divinity of Christ and the authenticity of his miracles, claiming them to be subsequent additions. Yet another factor assailing the Divinity Faculties in western universities was the advent of Darwinian theory.

Top left: Parker's Piece, the Univesity Arms Hotel (left) and the Hobbs pavilion, named after the great English cricketer, Jack Hobbs, who played here regularly

Middle left: Fenner's cricket ground, once graced by Peter May, David Sheppard and Ted Dexter

Bottom left: The ADC Theatre where John Cleese, Peter Cook, and Emma Thompson made their acting debuts

University sports and societies

The first college boat-houses appeared in 1825, and the first Boat Race against Oxford was held at Henley in 1829, transferring thereafter to Putney. The first 'Varsity' cricket match took place in 1827, in which Charles Wordsworth (Christ Church, Oxford), brother of the poet William, played a significant part, as he also did in the first Boat Race. In 1863 the rules of (Association) football were codified by academics meeting in Trinity College, before a trial game was held on the expanse of Parker's Piece in town. Voted an immediate success, it was soon followed by the first 'Varsity' football match, and the establishment of the Football Association in London. Rugby began in 1872 for those preferring something rougher.

As for societies, these too made their entry on the scene. The ADC Theatre is home to the Amateur Dramatic Society of the University; it has been on its current site since 1855 and is the oldest such society in Britain. In 1815 the debating society, named the Union Society, came into existence, before being temporarily closed two years later by the Vice-Chancellor Dr. James Wood (statue in St John's chapel) for its impudence in discussing government policy. It was reopened in 1821 by Christopher Wordsworth, Master of Trinity College and another brother of the poet, and it holds the distinction of being the oldest debating society in the world. The 'Apostles', so named as the society was limited to a membership of twelve, originated in 1820; continuous and tiresome lobbying by other students seeking entrance first drove the society underground in the 1850s, and a suggestion of secrecy has clung to it ever since. Unsurprisingly, perhaps, it would spawn the 20th century 'Cambridge spies' (see page 115).

Charles Darwin

Charles Darwin was never an atheist, but he became an agnostic—at a loss to know how to reconcile evolutionary theory with the biblical explanation of the origins of Creation. He first attended Edinburgh University where he found little interest in his medical studies. Leaving Edinburgh for Cambridge (Christ's College) he read theology and gained his degree. It was a modest one, since he had come to be influenced by J.S. Henslow and Adam Sedgwick, Professors respectively of Botany and Geology. Darwin, known as 'the man who walked with Henslow', spent hours looking at flowers in their natural habitat, whilst Sedgwick took him to examine rocks in north Wales.

In 1831 Darwin left on the 'Beagle' to circumnavigate the world. Wherever he went, he collected rocks, fossils, plants and skeletons. Arriving at ports where a ship was bound for England ahead of the Beagle's return, Darwin placed on board it a consignment of material for Henslow's attention and classification. Once he had returned in 1836, Darwin lived briefly in Cambridge before moving to Downe House in Kent where he spent twenty-three years collecting statistics to support his theories. He realised he held dynamite and hesitated to use it. In 1859, pressurised by others, he published his *Origin of Species* and the importance of the work was soon widely appreciated. Neither Henslow nor Sedgwick, however, would countenance Darwinian theory being taught at Cambridge; it only appeared after Sedgwick died in 1873. Darwin himself was married to a Christian and when he was dying his nurse was reading to him from Paul's Epistle to the Hebrews. Evolutionary theory had been around long before Darwin (his own grandfather, Erasmus Darwin, being interested in it), but it was Charles Darwin who explained the mechanism which drove it—natural selection. Others like T.H. Huxley deliberately used and abused the theory, aiming to destroy belief in the supernatural.

Above: '*Darwin's Shrine' in Christ's College, where he gained a theological degree and chased beetles, before circumnavigating the world (1831–1836)*

The Cambridge 'Triumvirate'

The Divinity Faculty attempted to meet this new threat. The 'Triumvirate' of three Fellows at Trinity College, J.B. Lightfoot, B.F. Westcott (both later Bishops of Durham) and F.J.A. Hort combined to write modern commentaries on the Pauline Epistles. Lightfoot implemented the construction of a new Divinity Faculty building, first proposed by William Selwyn, Professor of Theology and brother to George Augustus Selwyn, Bishop of New Zealand, in whose name Selwyn College was founded in 1879. The 'Triumvirate' also influenced the setting up of theological colleges (including Westcott House), first advocated by Charles Simeon. Between them, they installed stained glass depicting leading Christians through the ages in both Trinity and Emmanuel College chapels; Hort was by then a Fellow of Emmanuel. These aimed to promote Christianity to their captive student congregations. Their efforts were stiffened by the two American evangelical Moody and Sankey missions carried out in Britain and Cambridge in 1873 and again ten years later.

By then Charles Haddon Spurgeon, at the age of seventeen, had preached his first sermon at a small cottage in Teversham outside Cambridge. He attended St Andrew's Baptist Church in Cambridge, but being a nonconformist meant he was unable to take a university degree. He became the minister of Waterbeach Baptist Chapel, north-east of Cambridge, before moving to Southwark, where his preaching drew huge congregations. Such was the power of his voice that he once preached in the Crystal Palace before 23,654 people at the time of the Indian Mutiny, condemning the British for the situation that their misrule had created. One result of this was that after the mutineers finally surrendered on June 20, 1858, the British ended both the East India Company and the Mughal Empire, sending the deposed Emperor Bahadur Shah to exile in Burma. See in this series *Travel with C H Spurgeon* by Clive Anderson.

The Cavendish Laboratory

Others were also helping to promote science. William Whewell, Professor of Mineralogy and then of Theology, was also a classicist, linguist and scientist—the great polymath (much learning) and Master of

Above: The entrance to the new (now 'Old') Divinity School with the statues of Fisher (left) and Cranmer (right)

Trinity College. It was he who first coined the terms 'scientist', 'anode', and 'cathode'. George Gabriel Stokes (Pembroke College) was then the world's leading authority on optics. The astronomer John Couch Adams (St John's) predicted the orbit of a further planet (Neptune), based on the unexplained irregularities in the motion of Uranus, itself discovered by the older Herschel whose son was at St John's (see page 86).

Science, in fact, had become an examinable subject at Cambridge in 1851, through the influence of Prince Albert, Chancellor of the University (1847–1861). He was followed as Chancellor by William Cavendish, Duke of Devonshire, who in 1870 founded the world-famous Cavendish Laboratory which opened in 1874. Its first director was James Clerk Maxwell (Trinity College, and known for his 'Equations'), who is regarded as the link between

Above: C.H. Spurgeon

Newton and Einstein. The latter paid a visit to Cambridge in the 1920s, and was told: 'You have done great things, but you stand on Newton's shoulders'. 'No', replied Einstein, 'I stand on Maxwell's shoulders'. Maxwell died aged 48. Had he lived a normal span of life, it is estimated that he would have established the theory of special relativity at least a decade before Einstein. Maxwell was a great scientist but also a great Christian throughout his life. With the Chancellor's permission, he had the Cavendish family arms carved in Latin on the main entrance doors of the Laboratory, the words in Latin being from Psalm 111: 'Great are the works of the Lord, sought out by all those who take pleasure therein.' Here was a man who could see God's glory in the wonders of the world which science unveiled to him. In keeping with the 17th century scientists Maxwell believed that science and religion were totally compatible, and that the whole of humanity, not just 'those who take pleasure therein', should seek and find God through his Creation, something that Coverdale's faulty translation had failed to convey.

Clerk Maxwell was followed at the Cavendish by Lord Rayleigh, who discovered argon and inert gases. In turn he was succeeded by J.J. Thomson, who discovered the electron (the first part of the atom to be discovered), and under whom the brilliant young New Zealander, Ernest Rutherford was a student

Top: The statue of William Cavendish above the entrance

Above: The entrance to the old Cavendish Laboratory

(see page 112). It seemed that man was fast becoming 'the measure of all things'. Man, it was believed, would soon be able to know all there was to know about the world, and to control it. But then came the unexpected in the 20th century.

At the turn of the century in

Cambridge, a number of eminent literary figures were beginning to make their mark, including A.E. Housman, Lytton Strachey and Leonard Woolf, while the mathematician, philosopher and social reformer Bertrand Russell was collaborating with the mathematician A.N. Whitehead. One of Russell's students was Ludwig Wittgenstein, later Professor of Philosophy at Cambridge. All these were Trinity men.

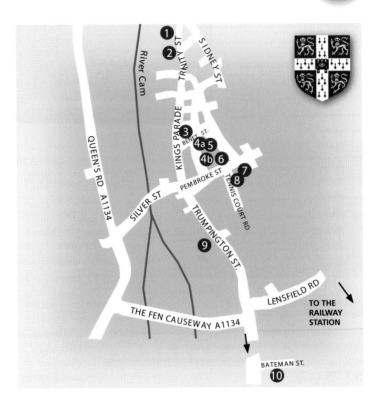

CAMBRIDGE: FOLLOWING THE 'ABOLITIONISTS' AND CAMBRIDGE SCIENTISTS

KEY

1 ST. JOHNS COLLEGE
2 TRINITY COLLEGE
3 THE EAGLE INN
   (AND ITS DNA PLAQUE)
4A THE OLD CAVENDISH
   LAB ENTRANCE

4B THE J.J. THOMSON
   PLAQUE
5 THE MAURICE WILKES
   PLAQUE
6 ZOOLOGY MUSEUM
7 GEOLOGY MUSEUM

8 ARCHAEOLOGICAL
   & ANTHROPOLOGY
   MUSEUM
9 FITZWILLIAM MUSEUM
10 UNIVERSITY BOTANIC
   GARDEN

TRAVEL INFORMATION

St John's College

St John's Street,
Cambridge, CB2 1TP
www.joh.cam.ac.uk
✆ 01223 338600

See details page 34.,
but this time visit the
statue of Clarkson as well
as that of Wilberforce
(outside and inside the
chapel respectively—as
per p.96 and 95 above).

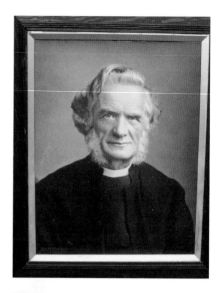

*Above: B.F. Westcott of Trinity
College, after whom Westcott
House theological college is
named*

*Left: The plaque in St John's
chapel to J.S. Henslow,
Professor of Botany and mentor
to Charles Darwin*

Trinity College

Trinity Street, Cambridge,
CB2 1TQ
www.trin.cam.ac.uk
✆ 01223 338400

Details as on page 92,
but on this occasion
spend time inspecting
the galaxy of stars
whose names feature
on the plaques in the
ante-chapel, scientists,
philosophers, and
mathematicians among
them, not to mention
the statues of others like
Macaulay, Tennyson and
Whewell (see above).

Descend King's Parade,
turning left into Bene't
Street. Note also the blue
circular plaque about
DNA on the outside front
wall of the Eagle. Crick
(Gonville & Caius) and
James Watson (Trinity
Hall) both worked at the
Cavendish and frequented
the Eagle.

Turn right down Free
School Lane. 150 yards
further, a sign on the wall
on your left announces
the Cavendish Laboratory.

(If you continue past the
oriel window, you will
find Thomson's plaque
against the wall). Go
through the entrance.
You are now on the New
Museums site. Note the
Cavendish motto inscribed
in Latin which faithfully
reflects the outlook of the
17th century scientists.
Continue straight on,
veering slightly left. 150
metres ahead is a brown
rectangular plaque to
Maurice Wilkes (King's
College), whose EDSAC
(Electronic Delayed

Storage Automatic Calculator) was the first digital computer to run commercially in 1949, based considerably on the machines used by the 'Enigma' code breakers. To the right lies the Zoological Museum (with Darwinian exhibits on display). If you exit the New Museum site onto Pembroke Street, turning left, you will reach the Downing site on the right, entry to which gives access to the Geology Museum (more Darwinian samples), and the Archaeological and Anthropological Museum (with exhibits stemming from Captain James Cook's exploration of the Pacific). Alternatively, if you've had enough of science and prefer art, turn right out of the New Museum site, proceed to Trumpington Street and turn left. The Fitzwilliam Museum will soon be on your right. (see page 78).

If you have energy enough, continue past the Royal Cambridge Hotel along Trumpington Road, turning left into Bateman Street. The highly regarded University Botanic Garden entrance will be on your right.

Above: The Cavendish family motto from Psalm 111 on the entrance doors of the 'Old' Cavendish Laboratory

Middle right 'The University Botanic Garden's 'Winter Garden'

Bottom right: The University Botanic Garden on its original site with King's chapel beyond

⑧ Science and religion— friends not foes

The growing myth of the 19th century which maintained that science and the power of human 'reason' would ultimately enable man to know everything there is to know about the world and to control it, was finally shattered by two world wars and the devastating economic crisis of the 1930s

Many important companies are actually 'embedded' within the University of Cambridge, such as Rolls Royce and Microsoft. Additionally, and located on numerous science parks, there are, within a thirty mile radius of the city centre, some 2500 companies working alongside the university, helping to advance high technology. The Science Park off Milton Road was founded in 1973 by Trinity College for research and development, and was followed soon after by the St John's College Innovation Park for the commercial development of new technological ideas, backed by venture capital. This overall development came to be called The Cambridge Phenomenon, and the region represents the biggest and fastest-growing concentration of hi-tech companies in Europe, referred to commonly as 'Silicon Fen' (taking its cue from 'Silicon Valley' in California). One third of the world-wide Human Genome Project is currently being carried out at Cambridge, primarily at neighbouring Hinxton at the Sanger Centre—named after the double

Nobel Prize winner, Fred Sanger of King's College. The fame of both city and University now ensures an annual influx of some four million tourists, and the crowds mingling in the streets are very international.

Facing page: *The new Centre for Mathematical Sciences with its futuristic pavilions*

Above: *The new Divinity Faculty building completed in 2000*

Left: The Human Genome Campus at the Sanger Centre, Hinxton, near Cambridge

Cambridge—city of science

Although, with the establishment of the Cavendish Laboratory, Cambridge acquired a reputation for physics, its reputation also now rests on biochemistry, materials science and computer technology. Following the work of Clerk Maxwell, Rayleigh and Thomson (see page 106), two scientists working at the Cavendish under Ernest Rutherford—Cockroft and Walton—split the atom using lithium. This was in 1932, and it was the first time the atom had been split intentionally anywhere—though done unintentionally in Manchester a few years before. Students and fellow physicists flocked to Rutherford, including Peter Kapitza (Russian), Niels Bohr (Danish; quantum theory), and the Englishmen Paul Dirac and James Chadwick (who later worked on the Manhattan Project developing the atomic bomb). All four were Nobel Prize winners. Rutherford's successor at the Cavendish was Lawrence Bragg whose name is associated with X-ray diffraction. Bragg's work was later of great importance to Francis Crick (Gonville and Caius) and James

Watson (Trinity Hall) who, together with Maurice Wilkins and Rosalind Franklin (London), unravelled DNA. The Cambridge pair later confessed the debt they also owed to Maurice Wilkes (King's College) who by then had built the world's first digital computer to run commercially (1949). His EDSAC (Electronic Delayed Storage Automatic Calculator—see also page 99) was vital to them as a 'number-crunching' facility which accelerated the processing of data. With so much talent in the sciences, though in other disciplines as well, it is hardly surprising that the tally of Cambridge Nobel Prize winners now stands at eighty one (2008). Where had Wilkes obtained his ideas for the design of his EDSAC? Not, in fact from Charles Babbage's mechanical computer (see page 99), except perhaps for punched data input, but from the machines invented at Bletchley Park, the 'Colossus' and 'Lorenz' machines which cracked the Enigma code used by the Germans in World War II. These machines had been developed by some of the finest brains in Britain—chess masters and mathematicians, men of genius like Alan Turing of King's College—who had the sheer power and flexibility of mind to produce

NEAR HERE
IN THE MATHEMATICAL LABORATORY
ON 6 MAY 1949
THE EDSAC COMPUTER
UILT BY MAURICE WILKES AND HIS TEAM
PERFORMED ITS FIRST CALCULATION.

15 APRIL 1999

such inventions from scratch. (See also under Charles Babbage, page 99).

The day in 1953, that Crick and Watson finally interpreted the double helix of DNA, they raced the short distance from the Cavendish to the Eagle pub, shouting, 'We've found the secret of life!' Had they? Does DNA account for the entire complexity of the human being? Are we nothing but atoms and molecules? Crick and Watson gravitated naturally back to the Eagle, for it was there that they passed much of their time—a genius needs the stimulation of a free exchange of ideas. It was also there that they gave the official account of their achievement to the gathered academics of the University. So, in 2003, on the 50th anniversary of discovering DNA, James Watson attended a Cambridge conference marking the event, and unveiled

the plaque on the front facade of the Eagle commemorating DNA.

It should never be forgotten, however, that before the mid 19th century and despite the individual achievements of Isaac Newton, William Harvey and others, Cambridge University was in no way noted for its science. Theology, the 'Queen of the Sciences', had long held sway. Theology and science should never be considered as foes but as friends. They both search for the 'Truth' through different but mutually inclusive approaches.

DNA Double Helix 1953
"The secret of life"
For decades the Eagle was the local pub for scientists from the nearby Cavendish Laboratory.
It was here on February 28th 1953 that Francis Crick and James Watson first announced their discovery of how DNA carries genetic information.
Unveiled by James Watson
25th April 2003

Top: *Maurice Wilkes' plaque on the New Museum site, positioned close to where he built the EDSAC*

Above: *The plaque to DNA on the Eagle facade, unveiled by James Watson in 2003*

Grantchester and the 'neo-pagans'

In Cambridge, the 20th century had opened with the neo-paganism of the Grantchester Group, an off-shoot of the Bloomsbury Group, a London-based set of Bohemian intellectuals. Its members often met in the Orchard Tea Gardens, Grantchester, which lie close upriver from Cambridge, and which Rupert Brooke immortalised in his poem 'The Old Vicarage, Grantchester' ('Stands the Church clock at ten to three? And is there honey still for tea?'). Other members of the group included the novelist E.M. Forster and the economist Maynard Keynes (who influenced F.D. Roosevelt's New Deal to assist the United States in the economic crisis of the 1930s); they were both King's College men (though Keynes was the bursar and held no university post); there were also the philosophers Bertrand Russell and Ludwig Wittgenstein (both Trinity College). The group included, furthermore, the writer Virginia Woolf and the artist Augustus John.

World War I and its aftermath

The cheerfully noisy and crowded colleges of the early century were soon reduced at the outbreak of the First World War to echoing shadows of their former selves, with fewer than half the usual number of students in residence in October 1914. Many Cambridge scientists, though far fewer than in World War II, were called away on war work. Soldiers, billeted in colleges—Nevile's Court (Trinity College) became a field hospital—or encamped in fields around the town, replaced many students, and college life was changed. As students came and went, departing for the front or returning wounded but capable of light study (special short courses being devised for them), compulsory chapel attendance was abolished; it was reintroduced at the end of the war, before finally dying out at Magdalene in 1933. Worcester was the last Oxford college to abolish it in 1954.

Inevitably the character of the University changed in the inter-war period. Faculty boards were established and funds allocated to them, whilst there was further construction of faculty

Above: *The Granta river at Grantchester, upstream from Cambridge*

buildings. The University's teaching role increased, whereas that of the colleges diminished. This represented a culture change which some regretted, especially when the sciences began to dominate the humanities. Scientific progress was not limited, however, to the Cavendish, and Frederick Gowland Hopkins (Trinity College) broke new ground in biochemistry, most famously with his discovery of vitamins. In 1929 he received the Nobel Prize for his contributions to physiology/ medicine.

The Scott Polar Research Institute was established in Lensfield Road with the largest polar archive collection in the world, whilst shrewd investments allowed the University Press to expand. The private house off Castle Street owned by Jim Ede, a modern art connoisseur (at one time a curator at the Tate Gallery), became the modern art museum known as Kettles Yard. The Folk Museum, displaying artefacts used by local artisans in the last 200 years, opened in 1936. With the completion of the University Library in 1934, one of the largest open access libraries in Europe which drew scholars from around the world, Cambridge could at last claim international status in reality as well as name. As for the students, they had supported the

authorities for the most part in the 1926 General Strike, especially when offered the chance to fulfil boyhood fantasies of driving trains and trams!

The immediately succeeding generations drew their inspiration in many cases from the romantic ideals of communism. Hitler's rise to power and the appearance of Jewish refugees negated any likelihood of a shift from the left, and Marxism became for many the only acceptable creed. Interest in things Russian continued, and it is scarcely surprising to find Cambridge producing the spies Blunt, Burgess, Maclean and Philby, all Trinity College alumni, the first two being members of the 'Apostles' (see page 103), a fact which inevitably veiled that organisation in further secrecy.

In other respects college life continued much the same. It featured in the writings of a Cambridge academic, for it was in 1930 that the novelist C.P. Snow,

Above:
The Scott Polar Research Institute

having been a student of Christ's College, became a Fellow of the same. His novel 'The Masters' (1951) stages the conflict aroused by the election of a new master in a Cambridge college.

World War II and beyond

Cambridge was not stripped of students in the second World War to the extent it had been in the first, nor as speedily, though the military were again present, some being billeted in colleges. There was however a different sort of invasion whereby government departments moved into several colleges, as did parts of London University—the London School of Economics and St Bartholomew's medical school for example. Cambridge dons also disappeared to Whitehall and Bletchley. When the war ended, many American servicemen, not immediately repatriated, took short courses at the temporarily inaugurated Bull College, converted from the old Bull Hotel. University life slowly returned to normal,

and the 1945 intake of students included the future naturalist and broadcaster David Attenborough (Clare College). The demand for post-graduate courses now grew enormously, and a decision was reached eventually to build more colleges to meet this demand. Churchill College was founded in 1960 with statutes requiring that 70% of its students were at all times scientists, mathematicians or engineers. Other colleges followed: Darwin (1964, based on the original home of George, the second son of Charles Darwin), Lucy Cavendish (1965), Clare Hall (1966), Wolfson (1973) and Robinson (1977). Other institutions were granted 'approved society' status before they attained full membership of the University (St Edmund's, Hughes Hall and, currently classified as an 'approved society', Homerton). Inevitably, the University's teaching staff increased to meet the rise in numbers: by 82% between 1938 and 1954. In the same period research student numbers rose by 164%.

The 'New Age'

Meanwhile the world-view held by Western society had altered fundamentally following two world wars and the 1930's global economic crash. The belief that man would ultimately know everything about the world and control it through science and 'human reason', which had characterised the previous two centuries, was seen to be groundless. The New Age was about to dawn with its rejection of all authority, and its insistence on relativism and pluralism.

After the war yet another museum appeared in Cambridge, namely The Whipple Museum of the History of Science. It stands at the bottom end of Free School Lane, being housed in the old assembly hall of the Perse School (now on a site off Hills Road). In the 1960s, Addenbrooke's Hospital, which had occupied a site alongside Trumpington Street since its mid 18th century inauguration (now the 'Judge Institute of Management Studies'), moved in stages to its current site on the southern outskirts of Cambridge where it has expanded ever since, and where it remains a teaching hospital linked to the University. When Max Perutz established the Medical Research Council Laboratory of Molecular Biology on a location adjacent to the new Addenbrooke's site, the personnel and techniques were largely drawn from the Cavendish. As for the Cambridge University Press,

the oldest publishing house in the world, it too moved from central Cambridge to its current location in Shaftesbury Road. Before then, however, Cambridge had attained 'city' status (1951) on the strength of its university.

Left: Darwin College and the old front door of the private house of George Darwin, son of the evolutionary naturalist

Top: Robinson College's mock castle appearance

Above: Fitzwilliam College and its spacious gardens

In time, Cambridge, and Great St Mary's in particular, was host to the evangelist Billy Graham, and later to Mother Teresa of Calcutta. The committed Christian, C.S. Lewis, who had been a Fellow of Magdalen College, Oxford, was persuaded to become a Fellow of Magdalene College, Cambridge, from 1954 to his death in 1963 His great friend J.R.R. Tolkien was instrumental in securing this move, a special post being created for him, that

C.S. LEWIS
1898 - 1963
*Professorial Fellow
of the College 1954-1963*

of Professor of Medieval and Renaissance English. (See in this series *Travel with C S Lewis* by Ronald Bresland).

In 1948, the first lady to obtain a degree was the late Queen Mother. She received an honorary degree in law from the then Chancellor, Jan Smuts. Since then women have taken degrees alongside men, and the student population is now 48% female, 52% male. All colleges bar three are mixed colleges, the last to accept the necessary change in its regulations being Magdalene College in 1988. The three exceptions are entirely for women. More recently Nelson Mandela was one of a number of celebrities to receive an honorary degree from the current Chancellor, Prince Philip.

The Theory of Everything

Fred Hoyle (Emmanuel College) taught mathematics in the University (1945–1958) before becoming its Plumian Professor of Astronomy and Experimental Philosophy. He propounded the one time influential 'steady state' theory of the universe, which proposed that the universe is uniform in space and unchanging in time, but which has since given way to the widely held 'Big Bang' theory of the universe's origins.

More recently the cosmologist Stephen Hawking, who graduated from Oxford and received his PhD from Cambridge, became Lucasian Professor of Mathematics at Cambridge, the very Chair once held by Isaac Newton. Hawking lives in Cambridge and is a Fellow of Gonville and Caius. His book *A Brief History of Time* appeared in 1988, claiming that he expected scientists in his own lifetime to discover the final theory: the 'Theory of Everything'. As he expressed it: 'Then we shall all, philosophers, scientists and just ordinary people, be able to take part in the discussion of the question of why it is that we and the universe exist. If we find the answer to that, it would be the ultimate triumph of human reason, for then we should know the mind of God.'

Aove: The plaque to C.S. Lewis in Magdalene College's ante-chapel

Above: Graduation Day

Above: Stephen Hawking, the cosmologist

Sixteen years later, in 2004, Stephen Hawking finally came to the conclusion that the pursuit of the 'Theory of Everything' was in vain. He reached this decision having revisited a proof produced by the Austro-American Kurt Goedel which has fascinated mathematical physicists for many decades. In 1931 Goedel had demonstrated that there are mathematical statements which no conceivable computer, however capacious, could settle. Crucially, philosophers of science have shown that what goes for mathematics goes for physics too. Their earlier objections, however, were drowned out by the hype surrounding Hawking's book. Eventually the connection between Goedel's theorem and the impossibility of the Theory of Everything became obvious to Hawking, and he went public on the matter in the newspapers. We should recognise that there are some things that lie beyond the capacity of science to understand.

A Brief History of Time had announced to an entire generation that the universe was both describable and explicable in terms of a single theory in physics. By implication, however, it downgraded all other forms of intellectual endeavour, including philosophy, theology, anthropology, literature, and history. It signalled the final triumph of science as the ultimate explanation. As John Cornwell (Director of the Science and Human Dimension Project at Jesus College) wrote in his book *Darwin's Angel*, itself one of several perceptive replies to Richard Dawkins' book *The God Delusion*: 'Your book, of course, goes one stage further: a Theory of Everything would signal, for you (Dawkins), the final fall of God and religion.' Cornwell wisely counsels Dawkins: 'In the meantime perhaps you too should pay a pilgrimage to Goedel's theorem.'

Cambridge: an evangelical Christian centre

Recent national surveys have indicated that Cambridge bucks the national trend in church attendance which remains substantially higher than the national average. However, what national surveys do not reflect has been the extremely healthy state of Cambridge's evangelical Christianity throughout the entire 20th century. Many of the city's central churches attract hundreds of university students, especially the Eden Baptist Church and St Andrew's the Great. The latter is strong on 'proclamation' of the word of God, whereas the former focuses on 'persuasion',

Above: A CICCU meeting in progress in the Eden Baptist Church, Cambridge

ie. 'apologetics'. The City Church remains strong as well. The work done by Christian Heritage at the Round Church has also benefited many students drawn to both its 'Big Picture' courses as well as to its summer courses in theology and 'apologetics'.

Cambridge Inter-Collegiate Christian Union

Cambridge's evangelical thrust has its origins in the Cambridge Inter-Collegiate Christian Union (CICCU) founded in 1877, which was itself inspired by the work of Charles Simeon (see page 91). CICCU was the first such student union in the world, leading to the institution of the OICCU at Oxford and soon afterwards to similar organisations in Canada and the United States. This 'movement'

has since become world-wide. Many missions to Cambridge have been connected with it, including several led by Dr Billy Graham and by Dr John Stott (Trinity College). Tyndale House was bought in 1942 by IVF (Inter-Varsity Fellowship) to be a Bible research centre; it remains such and is known internationally.

CICCU's continuous existence for 130 years is remarkable. It has retained its position despite pressures from the secular world, and contrary influences from both the High Church and from liberal

theologians. It did so by its members' evident desire to pass on to others the core beliefs of Christianity and to live their lives accordingly. Oliver Barclay, writing in his book *From Cambridge to the World* (2002), says of the CICCU 'How many organisations survive 125 changes of leadership in as many years? ... The continued existence of the CICCU was worthy of note in view of the odds against it. The example of CICCU members and their undying faith through 130 years surely gives the lie to current fashionable ideas.

Conclusion

This guide book has traced the reasons for the rise of Cambridge through the past millennium and more, from the Romans to research scientists via the Reformers. It is important to remember that this university was put on the map theologically, and therefore academically, by the Reformation in the 16th century, and that the 17th century scientists such as Galileo, Kepler and Newton, all did their science within a theological understanding of God's Creation. That understanding was not however shared by the 18th century society of the 'Enlightenment', nor the Modernist Society that followed in the 19th, even though scientists like Clerk Maxwell and J.J. Thomson found science totally compatible with their Christian convictions. Furthermore, many 'Simeonites' (the disciples of Charles Simeon) and others, inspired by the Evangelical Revival (including missionaries and social reformers such as Wilberforce), proclaimed the Gospel in word and in action. It seems, nonetheless, that dire warnings never suffice. Catastrophes are needed to make society take stock. It took the 20th century wars and the Wall Street crash to make man realise that 'man is not the measure of all things'.

Society then once more changed its thinking and its ways. In the 1960s, the New Age came on stage, featuring 'flower power' and 'Hippies', mysticism and drugs. No longer were students of Berkeley University, California, and of the Sorbonne, prepared to be treated like punched cards fed into a machine. People, at last, realised that there was something more to life, a third dimension. Life itself is meaningful, and human beings have dignity. At the time of writing, it seems that after decades of diminishing church congregations in Britain, the trend may be changing, if slowly. More people seem to acknowledge the compatibility of science with religion. A resurgence in evangelical church attendance in and around Cambridge, student led in most cases, is distinctly apparent and a source of hope for the future.

Cambridge must never lose its heritage and tradition that true Christianity and true science are wholly compatible. He who created both the world and the Christian faith said 'I am the way and the truth and the life' (John 14:6).

Above: *The Rubens' 'Adoration of the Magi' in King's College Chapel*

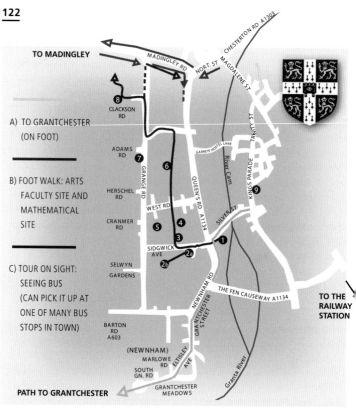

A) TO GRANTCHESTER (ON FOOT)

B) FOOT WALK: ARTS FACULTY SITE AND MATHEMATICAL SITE

C) TOUR ON SIGHT: SEEING BUS (CAN PICK IT UP AT ONE OF MANY BUS STOPS IN TOWN)

PATH TO GRANTCHESTER

CAMBRIDGE—A WALK ON THE WEST SIDE

KEY
1 DARWIN COLLEGE
2A NEWNHAM COLLEGE
    MAIN ENTRANCE
2B NEWNHAM COLLEGE

GARDENS
3 SIDGWICK AVE ARTS
   FACULTY SITE
4 THE LAW FACULTY
5 THE DIVINITY FACULTY

6 UNIVERSITY LIBRARY
7 ROBINSON COLLEGE
8 CLARKSON RD &
   MATHEMATICAL
   FACULTY SITE

TRAVEL INFORMATION

For countryside lovers, there is an attractive walk along the river in a south westerly direction from Newnham to Grantchester, barely two miles, where the old vicarage was once home to Rupert Brooke just before World War I. In his poem 'The Old Vicarage, Grantchester', he references the poet Lord Tennyson musing on the banks of Grantchester Mill Pond; the poem also refers to Byron's Pool upstream (Byron's haunt for ghostly midnight bathing), as also to the miller of Trumpington who appears in Chaucer's *Canterbury Tales*. Be sure to visit the old church immortalised in Brooke's poem. The small war memorial near the churchyard gate bears his name. Why not then discover the peace of the Orchard Tea Gardens where refreshments are available, as also leaflets on the 'Grantchester Group'? The small Rupert Brooke museum stands within the orchard.

Alternatively, on foot

Start outside Darwin College, originally home to four generations of the Darwin family, beginning with George, second son of Charles Darwin. Cross Queens' Road onto Sidgwick Avenue heading west.

Above: The Old Vicarage, Grantchester, where Rupert Brooke once lived

Go past Ridley Hall Theological College and proceed to the entrance of Newnham College to visit their gardens. Return to Sidgwick Avenue and continue west until level with the Arts Faculty site on your right. Walk through the site, taking in the modern architecture of several faculty buildings, notably Law (designed by Norman Foster) and Divinity (Edward Cullinan). Proceed past the front of the University Library (Sir Giles Gilbert Scott), turning left up Burrell's Walk and exiting on Grange Road close to Robinson College. If you proceed in a northerly direction, you will eventually reach Clarkson Road on your left, off which you will find the new Centre for Mathematical Sciences, a real eye-opener. If, however, you continue to Madingley Road and turn right, you will soon return to Queens' Road. The centre of town and various pubs and cafés are now within range, ready to refresh you.

Alternatively, by bus

Board one of the many open top sightseeing buses whose circuit takes in the developments in the north west of Cambridge. You will visit the American War Cemetery (the Wall of Remembrance includes the names of Glen Miller and Joseph Kennedy jnr, older brother of the American President). The route passes Churchill College (founded 1960) and the huge 'West Cambridge Development Site' on which the Cavendish Laboratory now stands, together with the University Computer Research Laboratory and, behind it, the Microsoft Laboratory. You then pass the Schlumberger Institute (a Franco-American organisation, developing new techniques for discovering and extracting gas and oil deposits), and the British Antarctic Survey where scientists first discovered the hole in the ozone layer, and where half the scientists each year spend half the year in Antarctica searching for mineral deposits.

Above: The Law Faculty building on the Arts Faculty site

TIMELINE

1209	Start of Cambridge University
1284	First college, Peterhouse, founded
1318	Pope's charter received by University
1446	King's Chapel foundation stone laid
1505/1511	Lady Margaret Beaufort founds Christ's and St. John's Colleges
1510–14	Erasmus at Cambridge
1513	Erasmus' *Novum Instrumentum* appears
1521	Luther's works destroyed (some saved)
1521	Little Germany at White Horse Inn
1533	Thomas Cranmer becomes Archbishop
1533	Henry VIII excommunicated
1535	Thomas More and John Fisher executed
1536–40	Dissolution of Monasteries
1546	Henry VIII founds Trinity College
1549	*Book of Common Prayer*
1555–6	Latimer, Ridley and Cranmer burned
1559	Puritanism starts in Cambridge
1584/1596	Emmanuel/Sidney Sussex founded as Puritan Colleges
1613	Subscription to the Thirty-nine Articles a condition for graduation
1628–40	Mass emigration to New England
1662	Isaac Newton enters Trinity College
1687	Isaac Newton's *Principia Mathematica*
1827	Jesus Lane Sunday School' started
1828-31	Darwin at Christ's College
1836	Death of C. Simeon, the great evangelical
1851	Natural Sciences first examined at Cambridge
1856	Cambridge Act. Overhaul of University's educational system
1870	Cavendish Laboratory founded
1871	University Tests (of allegiance to the C. of E.) abolished
1871/1873	Newnham/Girton colleges for women
1877	Birth of CICCU (Cambridge Inter Collegiate Christian Union)
1882	Fellows allowed to marry
1885	Departure of the 'Cambridge Seven' for China
2004	Stephen Hawking retracts earlier statement and now says man will never solve the 'Theory of Everything'

Index of travel information

Further Reading

GENERAL OVERVIEWS:

A.G. Dickens, *The English Reformation* (Fontana 1988)
Alister McGrath, *Reformation Thought* (Blackwell 2000)
William Haller, *The Rise of Puritanism* (Harper Torchbook 1957)
Elizabeth Leedham Green, *A Concise History of the University of Cambridge* (CUP 1996)
Ian Cooper, *The Cambridge Story: The Impact of Christianity in England* (Christian Heritage, Cambridge 2004)
(Edited by) **Sarah J. Ormrod**, *Cambridge Contributions* (CUP 1998)
Rita McWilliams Tullberg, *Women at Cambridge* (CUP 1998)
Oliver Barclay and Robert M. Horn, *From Cambridge to the World* (IVP 2002)

BIOGRAPHIES

Michael Jones and Malcolm Underwood, *The King's Mother* (CUP 1992).
Diarmaid MacCulloch, *Thomas Cranmer* (Yale 1997)
Brian Moynahan, *If God spare my life* (Little, Brown 2003) Reference William Tyndale
Hugh Evan Hopkins, *Charles Simeon of Cambridge* (Hodder and Stoughton 1977)
Ranald Macaulay, *Faith and Freedom* (Cambridge Heritage 2007) Reference William Wilberforce
C.H. Spurgeon, *C.H. Spurgeon: Autobiography 2. The Full Harvest* (Banner of Truth Trust 1973)
John Pollock, *The Cambridge Seven: The True Story of Ordinary Men used in No Ordinary Way* (Christian Focus Publications 2006)

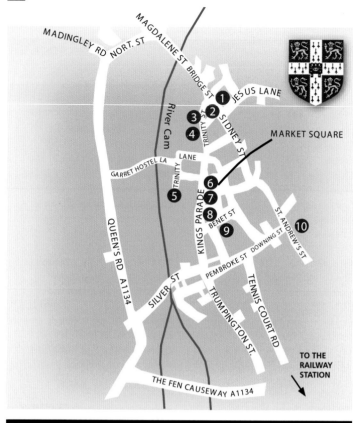

TOP TEN ATTRACTIONS

KEY
1 THE ROUND CHURCH
2 THE 'OLD DIVINITY SCHOOL'
3 ST JOHN'S COLLEGE

4 TRINITY COLLEGE
5 KING'S COLLEGE CHAPEL
6 GREAT ST MARY'S
7 ST EDWARD'S (KING & MARTYR) CHURCH

8 THE EAGLE INN
9 THE OLD CAVENDISH LABORATORY
10 EMMANUEL COLLEGE

Top ten attractions in Cambridge

For visitors who have only a few hours in Cambridge, the following top ten attractions are recommended. They all have strong associations with the city's Christian heritage.

The Church of the Holy Sepulchre (The Round Church)—an oratory or travellers' chapel, now home to Christian Heritage in Cambridge (see page 12)

The 'Old' Divinity School—with its nine statues of famous churchmen, including John Fisher, Erasmus, Thomas Cranmer, and Matthew Parker (see page 33)

St John's College—A Lady Margaret Beaufort foundation which was Wilberforce's college (see page 34)

Trinity College—where Isaac Newton did science within a religious understanding of God's Creation (see page 92)

King's College—with a chapel beyond compare, created by a godly king to reflect God's glory; the college where Charles Simeon influenced so many later clergy and missionaries (see pages 75)

Great St Mary's—the university church where the townspeople once seized the university's archives, where John Whitgift clashed with Thomas Cartwright, and outside which Luther's books were burned. It was here too that Billy Graham brought his crusade (see page 48)

St Edward's King and Martyr—the cradle of the English Reformation with Latimer's pulpit still in use (see page 41)

The 'Eagle'—where Wilberforce drank before his conversion, looking out on St Bene't's Church, the oldest building in Cambridgeshire (see page 64)

The 'Old' Cavendish Laboratory and the New Museums site—find the plaques to those who discovered the electron and designed the first digital computer; pass the site where they split the atom for the first time intentionally, and discover a whale, a Dodo, and the Darwin fish at the Zoological Museum (see page 105)

Emmanuel College—which produced so many great Puritans, many of whom led the emigrants to New England (see page 70)

Author

Having obtained his degree at Oxford, David Berkley taught modern languages and religious education. A lay minister, he retired to Cambridge in 1997, becoming an official guide for Christian Heritage, based at the Round Church, the University of the Third Age and also the Tourist Office. He is married to Tish and they have three children.

IMAGE ACKNOWLEDGEMENTS

The use of certain images is by kind permission of the following:

The Master and Fellows of Christ's College, the Master and Fellows of Clare College, the Master and Fellows of Corpus Christi College, the Master and Fellows of Downing College, the Master and Fellows of Emmanuel College, the Master and Fellows of Gonville and Caius College, the Master, Fellows and archivist, Dr Frances Willmoth of Jesus College, the Provost and Fellows of King's College, the Master and Fellows of Magdalene College, the Principal of Newnham College, the Master and Fellows of Pembroke College, the President and Fellows of Queens' College, the Master and Fellows of St John's College, the Master and Fellows of Sidney Sussex College, the Master and Fellows of Trinity College, the Master and Fellows of Trinity Hall, and The Principal of Westcott House.

The use of certain other images is by kind permission of: The Communications Services Department of the University, and Christian Heritage (The Round Church, Cambridge).

Photograph reproductions by kind assistance of PANDIS (Photographic and Illustration Service).

The author also wishes to express his gratitude to many members of Christian Heritage, in particular Ian Cooper for his encouragement and initial proof-reading, and Martin Lown for the technical assistance provided on numerous occasions.

CAMBRIDGE

KEY

COLLEGES

1 MAGDALENE
2 ST JOHN'S
3 TRINITY (COLLEGE)
4 TRINITY (HALL)
5 CLARE
6 SIDNEY SUSSEX
7 GONVILE & CAIUS
8 KING'S
9 JESUS
10 WESLEY METHODIST
   (THEOLOGICAL)
11 WESTCOTT HOUSE
   (THEOLOGICAL)
12 CHRIST'S
13 EMMANUEL
14 CORPUS CHRISTI
15 ST CATHERINE'S
16 PEMBROKE
17 PETERHOUSE
18 QUEEN'S
19 DARWIN
20 RIDLEY HALL
   (THEOLOGICAL)
21 NEWNHAM
22 ROBINSON
23 DOWNING

OTHER SITES OF INTEREST

1 CASTLE MOUND/ SHIRE
  HALL
2 ST PETER'S
3 ST GILES'
4 THE PICKEREL INN
5 QUAYSIDE/MAGDALENE
  BRIDGE
6 THE ROUND CHURCH
7 'OLD DIVINITY SCHOOL'
8 'OLD SCHOOLS'/ THE
  ORIGINAL DIVINITY
  SCHOOL
9 GREAT ST MARY'S
10 HOLY TRINITY
11 MARKET HILL (SQUARE)
12 ST EDWARD'S
13 ST ANDREW'S THE GREAT
14 'LITTLE GERMANY'
   PLAQUE
15 ST BENET'S
16 THE EAGLE INN
17 SITE OF AUSTIN FRIARS'
   RELIGIOUS HOUSE
18 THE CAVENDISH
   LABORATORY
19 EDSAC PLAQUE
20 ST BOTULPH'S
21 EMMANUEL U.R.C.
22 LITTLE ST MARY'S
23 FITZWILLIAM MUSEUM
24 OLD ADDENBROOKE'S
   HOSPITAL
25 HOBSON'S CONDUIT
   (FOUNTAIN)
26 ZOOLOGY MUSEUM
27 GEOLOGY MUSEUM
28 ARCHEOLOGY &
   ANTHROPOLOGY
   MUSEUM
29 THE COPPER KETTLE
30 DON PASQUALE